155
Office Shortcuts
and Time Savers
for the Secretary

155 OFFICE SHORTCUTS AND

PARKER PUBLISHING COMPANY, INC.
West Nyack, N.Y.

by the Editorial Staff of
Parker Publishing Company

TIME SAVERS
FOR THE SECRETARY

155 Office Shortcuts and Time Savers for the Secretary, the Editorial Staff of Parker Publishing Co.

© 1964 BY

PARKER PUBLISHING COMPANY, INC.

WEST NYACK, N. Y.

ALL RIGHTS RESERVED. NO PART OF THIS BOOK MAY BE REPRODUCED IN ANY FORM, BY MIMEOGRAPH OR ANY OTHER MEANS, WITHOUT PERMISSION IN WRITING FROM THE PUBLISHER.

LIBRARY OF CONGRESS
CATALOG CARD NUMBER : 64-19988

Twelfth Printing . . . . . November, 1975

PRINTED IN THE UNITED STATES OF AMERICA

63543—B&P

Streamlining Your Work Day

A good deal of the secretary's day is taken up with dictation, typing, filing, and the like. Whether you are experienced or just out of school, you want to know how you can save time on these daily assignments. This booklet is full of tips that will help you get your work completed faster and with less effort.

Most routine office tasks have short cuts. Too often the secretary gets in the habit of performing a job in one fashion, and fails to realize there may be a quicker and easier method in the offing. You may be surprised to find that even the simplest jobs can waste precious minutes. For example, when you add long columns of figures, do you try to keep a running total in your head? Dividing the long column into short sections would considerably lessen the time spent on this chore. Are you continually going through your files checking on material to be followed up? Look at the tips in our filing section to find the fast, easy way to handle follow-up material.

Another point to remember is that your work is more interesting when you know the short cuts. The secretary who has to count lines and measure margins every time she types a report soon becomes bored with these time consuming procedures. If you use the guide sheet suggested in this booklet, you will be able to set up a report in seconds and go right on with your typing.

Start your streamlining today. There are more than one hundred and fifty tips waiting in the following pages to shorten your work day.

Contents

1. **Typing Tips** . . . 1
   Centering and spacing made easy
   Tips on preparing form letters
   Quick ways to handle envelopes
   Carbon shortcuts
   Speedy ways to make corrections
   Electric typewriter time savers

2. **Correspondence Shortcuts** . . . 15
   Dictation and transcription shortcuts
   Quick ways to process mail
   Streamlining with forms

3. **Faster Filing and Finding Tips** . . . 25
   Ways to make finding easier
   How to save time in setting up files
   Follow-up files
   Office calendars

4. **The Telephone as a Timesaver** . . . 41
   Organizing your telephone calls to save time
   Keeping a telephone and address book
   Special equipment makes telephoning easier

5. **Office Machines Can Save Work** . . . 45
   Dictating machines save time for you and your executive
   Save extra typing with your office copier
   Cut down filing chores with microfilm

6. **Math Shortcuts** . . . 53
   Shortcut methods of adding, subtracting and multiplying
   Using factors for quick calculations

7. **Where to Find the Answer** . . . 75
   Books that can save you time
   Atlases, dictionaries, business guide books and periodicals

8. **Miscellaneous Time Savers** . . . 85
   Quick ways to collate, count cards, correct stencils, handle supplies and process papers

1
Typing Tips

A GOOD PART OF YOUR DAY IS SPENT AT THE TYPEwriter. How much of this time is being wasted? You may be surprised at the answer. Study these tips and see if you haven't been doing things the hard way.

Centering and spacing made easy How much time do you waste counting and recounting lines to make sure you have the same number on each page? You can save this time with a simple chart.

On a 9 by 12 inch sheet of paper, on the right hand margin, make a scale indicating line spacing for your typewriter. Place the chart in back of the sheet of paper on which you are typing, so that the scale shows on the right. Note the number at which you stop typing on the first page, and end each succeeding page on the same number. This method is probably most helpful when you are typing handwritten notes. (The chart is illustrated on page 2).

Other ways to get the same number of lines on each page Some typewriters have a numbered strip at the left edge of the platen. With this kind of machine, do the following:

1. Feed each page into the machine in alignment with the number one.

2. Note the number on which you begin typing the first line of your model page. Start all pages on the

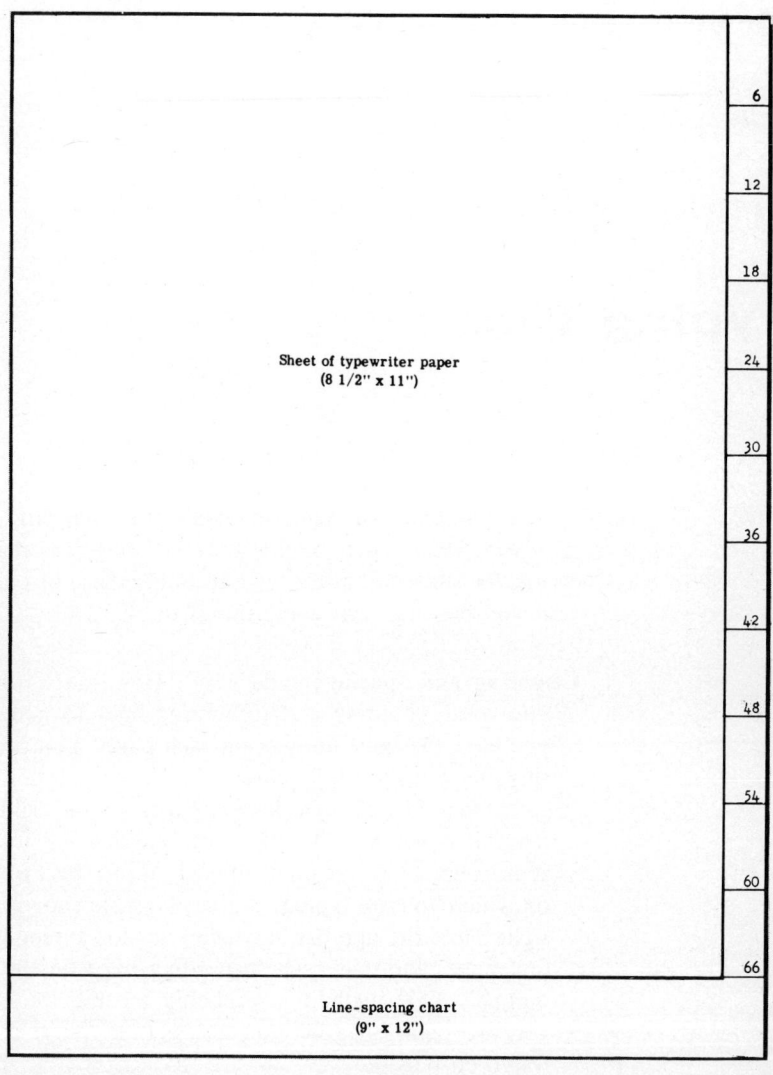

same number.

3. Note the number on which you type the last line of the page. Finish all pages on the same number.

If your typewriter doesn't have the numbered strip you may try this method:

1. Type the first page.
2. Lightly mark the next sheet with pencil, indicating the first line by having your pencil mark in line with the bottom edge of the first line of type. You can align your machine on this mark.

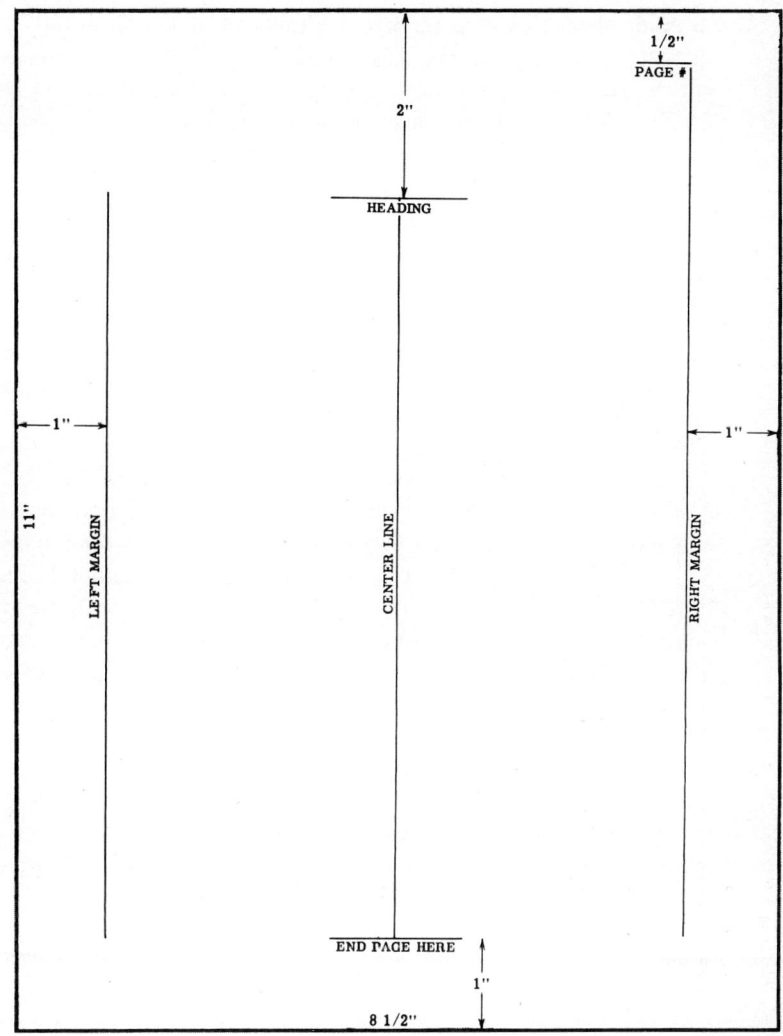

3. Place a second pencil mark about four lines before the final line of type so that you can see the pencil mark as it comes out of the carriage. This tells you there are four lines remaining to complete the page.

Let the tabulator save you time The tabulator is not for charts and tables alone; it can save you time when typing letters. Set the tabulator for paragraph indentations, the date line, and the closing and signature line. Unless you are using full block style, this idea will shorten a routine chore. Properly set, the tabulator also provides a speedy short cut when you are typing subheadings and quoted material.

Use a guide sheet to set up reports A uniform style concerning margins, headings, and page numbers is usually employed for certain kinds of reports. Here is a quick way to keep these items consistent.
    First of all you need a chart similar to the one on page 3. Mark the outlines of the margins, chapter titles, and so on. The guide lines must be dark enough to be seen through the original page. Insert the guide sheet into the typewriter behind the paper on which you are going to type. Then line up your carbons in normal fashion behind the guide sheet.

A quick way to set margins The quickest way to set margins is by estimating, not counting spaces. Here are some tips to help you along.
    1. *Keep your paper guide in the same place.* This makes it easier to use your typewriter scale.
    2. *Put your letters into classifications.* All letters should be classified as short, medium, or long. Once you have set up your margins for each category, it only takes a few seconds to set up a letter for typing.
    3. *Don't forget insertions.* Before you make any estimate, check for insertions. You may have estimated for a short letter, only to find you have a notation to insert four paragraphs from another source. Try putting a check mark in the margin next to letters that have insertions.
    4. *Don't forget attention lines.* Before classifying a letter you are about to type, check to see if it has an attention or subject line, or even both. This can make a difference in your spacing.

Large totals can be typed in narrow columns Start out by typing the total in the first column so that the extra digits extend over the left line of the column. Space down one line and repeat the procedure for each succeeding column. This avoids crowding and keeps your work neat and legible.
    Example:

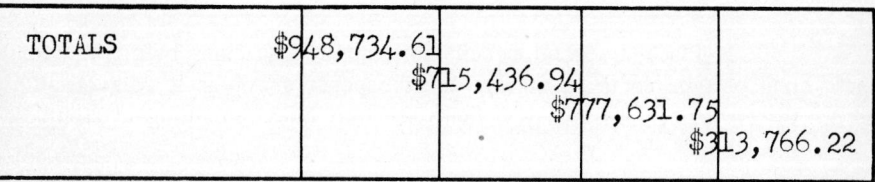

Tips on preparing form letters Here are four ideas that can save you time when preparing form letters.
    1. *Don't waste time proofreading each copy.* As you type each new

letter, use the preceding letter as your guide; you'll be proofreading the last copy while you type the next. The only danger here is that you may omit a line in one copy and follow suit with the rest. Therefore, be sure to register the lines in each letter you type against the lines in the original letter.

2. *Positioning addresses quickly and correctly.* While most form letters are run off on a duplicating machine, you will probably have to type in the addresses yourself. When preparing the master copy of the letter to be duplicated, make a mark with a pin point to signal where you should start the addresses. A slight impression will be duplicated on every letter, thereby simplifying the process of filling in the addresses.

3. *When you have to leave additional space, leave it at the top.* When space is to be left on a form letter for the insertion of a personal paragraph, leave the space at the top rather than the bottom of the letter, when you set up the master letter. This short cut saves time for two reasons. First, you don't have to space so far down in order to type the additional material. Second, the typewriter grips the paper better at the top, thereby eliminating the need to shift and adjust. Naturally, you can use this trick only if the paragraph to be inserted will sound right as the opening paragraph.

4. *An easy way of calling attention to special paragraphs.* When you want to draw attention to a paragraph on the form that is being mailed with a letter, you mark the particular section with an "X," and in the body of the accompanying letter you type "Please refer to the paragraph marked 'X' on the enclosed form." The disadvantage of this is that you waste a great deal of time lining up the proper paragraph in order to place an X opposite it, especially when there are carbon copies to be properly aligned also.

A better method is to number the paragraphs of the form when you are typing the original stencil. Then all you have to do in the accompanying letter is type "Please refer to Paragraph Number 1 on the enclosed form."

Get rid of those dark lines and smudges on your letters When the rubber wheels on the paper bail of your typewriter become dirty or worn they leave smudges on your letters and reports. Cover the wheels with cellophane tape. This keeps your papers clean and also helps them move through the bail more smoothly.

To avoid smudges when drawing lines with an ink pen, put a blotter under the ruler, lined up with edge of ruler.

How to type post cards in a jiffy Both the address and message can be typed without turning the card by hand, if you can master a trick on a typewriter that may take some practice. Give the platen a quick turn after typing one side of the card. If you do it right, the card flips back, strikes the paper table, and drops into position to type the other side.

Type above and below the line without having to realign original work You may find yourself typing such things as chemical formulas, or perhaps references to footnotes, which go either above or below the line. The trick is to use the ratchet detent lever, not the variable line spacer, to release the roller. The platen can be revolved to any point to write the subscripts or other characters. When the lever is engaged again you will be able to return the platen to the same line on which you were originally typing.

- **remember** The detent lever is not the same as the variable line spacer. The variable line spacer permits you to revolve the platen freely, but does not permit you to return the platen automatically to the same relative spacing position.

A quick way to type your envelopes with your letters When typing correspondence, drop the envelope in your machine between the letter and the platen before removing the letter. If you insert the envelope to the left of your paper guide, and the margins you have been using for the letter are wide enough, you may be able to use your left margin stop (already set) for typing the envelope.

Short cut for typing envelopes Fold a piece of heavy paper through the center. Insert the folded end into the roller of the typewriter and roll it through until it extends about an inch above the front scale.

Now insert the envelope at the front of the roller, behind the folded paper. (The flap of the envelope should be at the top, turned away from you.) Turn the roller back as many spaces as you need to bring the envelope to the proper position for addressing. Type the address and then turn the roller up enough spaces for you to lift out the envelope. The folded paper is then in place for the next insertion.

Save time by preparing envelopes in advance Take some time once a month to type a batch of envelopes to people and companies with whom your employer corresponds regularly. Then, when you have one of those last minute letters, one part of your job is already done.

Save time with window envelopes Window envelopes mean you don't have to type the address twice. In addition, you no longer have to worry about envelopes getting switched in the mail rush and letters going to the wrong people. Finally, your employer will no longer be hampered by envelopes attached to letters he has to sign.

It isn't necessary to type an unbalanced letter to be sure that the address will show through a window envelope. A letter using standard spacing and folded on the top line of the body of the letter will fit a window envelope.

Type small labels using both hands Here is a way you can avoid holding the label with one hand and having to do all the typing with the other. Make a horizontal pleat about an inch deep in a sheet of paper. Feed the sheet of paper into the machine in the regular way, maintaining the pleat so the folded edge will be up when the material is in writing position. The pleat forms a pocket. When the pocket appears at the front of your platen, insert the label, or several of them, in the pocket. Feed all the material back so that you can type on the label.

Sheet labels can be typed faster Typing single labels is a time-consuming job. With sheet labels you can type faster and the machine grips them better. All you do is insert the sheet and type. Since the sheets are perforated for easy tearing, the labels can be quickly separated when you are through typing. More time is saved in typing than you use to separate the labels.

How to type rush jobs with work still in the typewriter Let's say you have a letter—with carbons—in the typewriter, and you are asked to type out a rush telegram or memo. First, release the roller with the ratchet detent lever, and back feed the paper already in the typewriter until the paper shows a top margin of about two inches. Insert the first sheet of telegram or memo against the paper table, behind the material that is already in the machine, so that it will come out on top. For carbon copies, insert the second sheet of the telegram against the coated side of the carbon paper (between the carbon and the second sheet of your letter), and so on.

- *important* You must insert a sheet of paper for each carbon in your typewriter to prevent the rush typing from showing on the carbon copies of your original work. If you need more copies of the telegram or memo than there are carbons in the work you already have in your machine, just insert additional carbon sheets in the usual manner.

Now turn the platen knob so that the telegram or memo blanks are in position to be typed. Return the ratchet detent lever to normal position. After typing the rush job, back feed until it may be removed from the machine. Forward feed to where you stopped your other work and continue.

How to type on carbon copies only   To type something only on certain copies of a letter, place a small piece of paper over the original letter and an additional piece over each of the carbons on which you do not want the notation to appear. Type the message and remove the extra pieces of paper. The message appears only on those copies before which you did not insert a piece of paper.

This method may produce a slight indentation on the original page. To avoid this you may try one of the following methods:

Typing information on the top of carbon copies. Insert paper in the usual way. Use paper release lever to free paper. Now move the carbon pack an inch or so above the original and return the paper release lever to the "tight" position. Feed the material back and type in the information. Then feed material forward again. Use the paper release lever and align the original with the carbon pack. Return the paper release lever to "tight" position and you are ready to type your letter.

Typing information on the bottom of carbon copies. Position the machine exactly where you want material to appear. Use the paper release lever and slip the original out of the machine without disturbing the carbon pack, engage the paper release lever, and start typing.

- **remember**   Position the machine before removing the original, because after the original is removed the first piece of carbon covers up the carbon copy of the letter you have typed. You may smudge the copy and draw the others out of alignment if you try to pull out the first carbon sheet.

You don't have to separate carbons one copy at a time   When setting up your correspondence, adjust carbons so they protrude slightly from the bottom of the writing paper. Use carbon paper with one corner cut off at the bottom (you can buy it that way). Then hold the corner of the writing paper where the carbons have been cut and withdraw the carbons.

Keep your carbons from creasing   Put a sheet of heavy paper behind the carbon pack. This keeps the papers from wrinkling. If you still get creases in your carbon, have a repairman check the roller in your typewriter. Sometimes the roller is too close to the paper rest, which makes it difficult for the papers to fit into the machine.

Throw away your old carbon paper How much time do you waste sorting through used carbon paper debating whether you can still use it? There is a much simpler and quicker method of determining when your carbon has outlived its usefulness. Each time you use a piece of carbon, put a small nick, or punch a hole, along the edge. When you decide the carbon is no longer useful, count the nicks or holes down the side. Suppose there are ten. Now you know that as soon as you have ten nicks on a carbon it is time to throw it away.

A simple way to make carbon copies Would you like to save stationery and filing space with carbon copies? The next time you answer a letter, make the first carbon on the opposite side of the letter itself. Then you have your original and file copy on one sheet. This makes for easier filing and finding.

When you are typing material that runs more than one page, the procedure is slightly different. Set up your carbon copies in the usual manner for the first sheet. When you come to the second sheet, use the back of the first sheet for your file copy.

- *note* Be sure your executive approves of this idea before putting it into practice.

A quick way to change colors while typing Sometimes you find you would like to use a different color for a portion of a chart or letter. Often you would prefer a color other than the two on your typewriter ribbon. You can make the desired change quickly and easily. First, set the typewriter as if you were making a stencil. Then hold a piece of colored carbon at the printing point.

As a rule your carbon copies do not have to reflect the change in color. If you wish to show it, however, simply insert a piece of colored carbon under your regular carbon paper and type.

A series of small cards can be chain fed Type the first card and then feed backwards until the card has a top margin of about three-quarters of an inch. Insert the next card so that the bottom of it will be held in place by the card just completed. Then feed back again until the new card is in position to type. Thus, each succeeding card is held in place by the card preceding it.

Envelopes can be typed faster by chain feeding Use the same system outlined above. The envelopes will pile up on the paper table in the same order in which they are typed. This saves you the trouble of re-sorting them.

When the flap on an envelope you type is so thick or so wide that the typing is ragged, it may be better to chain feed from the back of the platen. To do this, open the flap of the next envelope to be typed and insert it between the first envelope and the paper table, before removing the first envelope. A twirl of the platen knob removes one envelope and automatically brings the next one into position to be typed. Prepare your envelopes in chains of three when using this system, if you are typing several envelopes.

Numerous sheets will fit into your typewriter   Do you find yourself typing the same assignment twice because you can't fit all the copies into your machine at the same time? The next time you run into this problem try one of these tips.

When you have a medium size pack, put the paper in the machine without the carbon. Roll the platen up just enough to hold the paper in place. Now insert the carbons one by one, making sure the shiny or carbon side faces you. Roll back into position for typing.

When you have a very large pack, use the following device. Fold a 6 by 8½ inch strip of Manila tag (an old file folder will do) across the center, lengthwise. Cut three U-shaped slots across the upper half of the folded strip, about one-half inch from the crease. Lift up and bend backward the tongues formed by the slots.

Insert the assembled sheets of paper in the folded strip. Feed the tongues from the U-slots into the typewriter. The platen grasps them more readily than it does a thick pack of paper. Remove the folded strip before beginning to type.

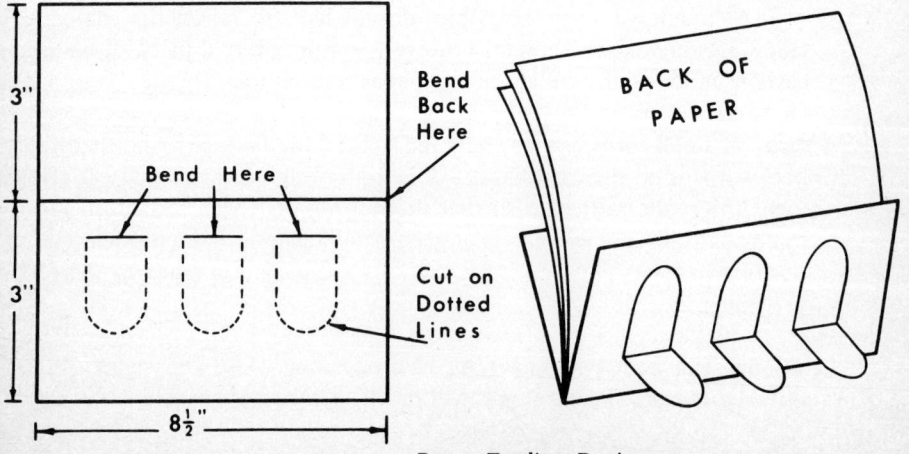

Paper Feeding Device

A quick way to draw lines with your typewriter Unless you have an electric typewriter with an automatic underscore, drawing lines can be a time-consuming job. Here are two ways you can speed up the process.

Horizontal lines. To draw horizontal lines, insert a pencil (or ball point pen) in the fork of the ribbon guide, not through the ribbon. Using the carriage release, move the carriage across the paper until the line is completed.

Vertical lines. To draw vertical lines, release the platen either with the variable line spacer or the automatic line finder (ratchet detent lever). Roll the platen up while holding a pencil (or ball point pen) firmly in the fork of the ribbon guide at the desired spot, not through the ribbon.

- *note* If you have a new machine there is probably a special place to insert a pencil when drawing lines, but inserting the pencil in the fork of the ribbon guide is satisfactory if your typewriter does not have this extra convenience.

Typing special characters not on your machine Standard characters can be overprinted to form special characters that may not be on your keyboard:

¶	paragraph mark	P and l
÷	division sign	colon and hyphen
£	Pound Sterling sign	f and t, or L and f
ç	Cedilla beneath "c"	c and comma
!	exclamation point	apostrophe and period
=	equation sign	Hyphen--use ratchet detent lever and turn platen slightly
[ ]	brackets	underscore and diagonal

- *note* One character can be typed over another without backspacing by holding down the space bar as you type, except when using an electric machine with an automatic space bar.

Don't remove paper from typewriter for last line corrections This only means time wasted while you realign all the carbon copies. When you make an error in the last line simply feed the sheet back until the bottom edge comes out of the platen far enough to erase on. Make the erasure and turn the page back into position. **Remember,** use your ratchet detent lever when feeding sheets back and forth, so you can return to the same line.

Erase neatly and save retyping   Use erasers, a hard one and a soft one, to make neat erasures. Work with the soft eraser first to remove surface ink, then use the hard eraser to remove imbedded ink. Finally, use the soft eraser again to smooth off the surface.

You can disguise an erasure by lightly rubbing a piece of chalk or an aspirin tablet over the corrected error. Dust it off with a clean brush and type in the correction.

Another tip: many secretaries keep their typing erasers on a string, tied to the typewriter. This saves hunting under papers on the desk or looking in drawers.

A quick way to align papers for corrections   Frequently you won't notice a typing error until after you have removed the paper from the typewriter. Reinserting the material so it is properly aligned can be a job. Here is a tip to help you manage it.

Reinsert the paper and operate the paper release. Move the work around till you have lined up a straight letter (1 is good) above a vertical marking on the typewriter scale. Now, set your machine for stencil typing and type over one of the letters you already have in print. Check to see if the imprint is aligned with the original letter. Once you get the two imprints aligned, you are ready to make the correction.

Two things to remember:

1. It's best to type the test letter on scrap paper first once or twice; even though the setting is on stencil, some ink will be left on the face of the type.

2. If the correction is extensive, make sure the left margin of the work is lined up exactly as it was.

Insert omitted letters in words quickly and easily   A forgotten letter may be inserted into a word without disturbing a whole line of type. Erase the whole word first. Then fix the carriage so that the space immediately following the last letter of the preceding word is at the exact printing point. Hold down the space bar while you strike the first letter of the word. Release the space bar and depress it again while striking the second letter.

Follow this procedure until the word is completed. There will be a partial space between the corrected word and the words immediately preceding and immediately following it. This spacing is barely noticeable and the rest of the line is not affected. If you have an electric typewriter without a half-space key, you will have to hold the carriage back manually and estimate the partial spacing.

A quick way to correct bound or stapled material Make the erasure. Then insert a blank sheet of paper in the typewriter in normal fashion. When it protrudes about an inch above the platen, insert between it and the platen the unbound edge of the sheet to be corrected. Now turn the platen toward you until the typewriter grips the sheet to be corrected. Adjust the bound sheet to the proper position for making the correction.

- *important* Corrections cannot be made on pages that are bound at the side, without unfastening them.

A newer and quicker way to clean your typewriter Get a kind of paper with chemically treated fibers that pick up lint and dirt. Insert it into your typewriter as you would an ordinary sheet of paper. Set the machine to stencil and strike each key about five times. The sheets are not expensive and the saving of time and effort is great.

Shortcuts for the girl with an electric typewriter Here are five extra ideas just for electric typewriters.

1. *A quick way to type characters beneath each other.* When you have to type quotation marks to indicate ditto marks down the page, do you waste time lining each one separately? Here is how you can short cut this kind of job. Depress the character and then depress the backspace key and the carriage return simultaneously. The machine will be in position for you to repeat the procedure. To speed this process (on most models), use the forefinger and thumb of your right hand to touch the backspace and carriage return keys and use the forefinger of your left hand to depress the particular key you wish to type.

2. *Speed up your typing with the automatic underscore key.* When an electric typewriter has this key, all you have to do is touch it and it continues to type until you remove your finger. You can underscore backwards by depressing the backspace and underscore keys at the same time. This saves time when you type headings. You no longer have to return the carriage to underscore; after typing the heading, immediately underscore backwards.

3. *Save time with partial carriage return.* When you are typing columns of figures, do you waste time bringing the carriage all the way back to the left margin with each new line? Save time with a partial carriage return by touching the carriage return key and then the tabulator

key. This short cut can be perfected by touching the tabulator key just after your carriage has passed the set tabulator stop on its way back to the left margin. With just a little practice you can make this procedure a real time saver.

4. *A tip on typing technique.* Learn to roll your fingers over the keys. With an electric typewriter the pressure you exert on the keys has no effect on the appearance of your work. Nor does typing in a set pattern accomplish anything, since rhythm is never reflected in your finished typing. If you can type some combinations of letters faster than others, do so.

5. *Switching over from a manual to an electric typewriter.* The difference in the two types of machine is the touch. Take a few minutes to become acquainted with your new typewriter and prevent time-wasting mistakes later on. First move the on-off lever of your electric machine to the half-way ON position. No electricity should be coming through the typewriter, but the keys will go down.

Type a simple practice sentence or exercise twenty times. The keys will go down just as though you were actually typing. Now turn the machine on and type the sentence or exercise once more.

Perhaps your machine can be set for touch so that the keyboard can have the "stiffness" you prefer. This setting doesn't affect the depth or darkness of the impression.

2

Correspondence Shortcuts

How much of your day is taken up with dictation, transcription, and incoming and outgoing mail? These basic tasks often mean time wasted in needless routine. You get in the habit of doing something one way and never stop to think that there may be a shorter method. This section has all the tips you need to start your streamlining.

Transcribe your notes as soon as possible Ideally you should transcribe your shorthand notes immediately after your employer stops dictating. Of course this isn't always possible, but don't let them go any longer than is absolutely necessary. Undoubtedly you already know how fast you can forget the details in an outline. Then you have to go back to your employer, who has also forgotten by this time exactly what he said.

Check your notes right away When you can't go right from dictation to transcription, you might try the following suggestion. As soon as you leave your boss' office take a few minutes to read over your notes. If anything isn't clear you can check it right away. This also gives you a chance to check on the rush items in your notes.

Try to set aside a specific time for dictation Does your boss dictate a few letters at a time? Perhaps you could tactfully suggest that he set aside an hour or so every morning for dictation. Point out how this means less interruptions for him (and you) during the day. It also means that you can get out all of his letters on the same day.

When your employer is ready to dictate—be prepared Check your supplies every morning. When your employer is ready to start dictating, you should not be running around looking for pencils or a fresh notebook. Keep your supplies up to date at all times. When you keep the boss waiting, you are wasting his time as well as your own.

Gather needed correspondence before you start transcription How many times have you begun your transcription and had to stop and dig out related correspondence? Make sure you have the necessary files and enclosures *before* you sit down to type. Also see that it is arranged in the same order as your notes. Organization beforehand will speed you through any task.

When you have several insertions in your notebook Do you have trouble deciding which insertion goes where when you are transcribing? To avoid this confusion, number your insertions and place matching numbers in the material at the point where the insertion is to be made. In this fashion you can match up notes and insertions at a glance.

Find letters fast in your notebook Do you flip pages frantically looking for a date or can you turn to the right page in a few seconds? It all depends on how you date your work. Placing the date at the bottom of each page enables you to locate particular letters in a flash.

A quick way to flip pages When you come to the bottom of the page in your notebook, do you lose a sentence while trying to flip over to the next sheet? There is a quick, easy way to for you to keep your work flowing smoothly from page to page. First put a rubber finger on your left thumb. Place your thumb at the middle of the page with the rest of your fingers beneath the pad. As you go past the center of the page, move your thumb upward, causing the paper to curl at the top of the notebook. At the same time move your index finger under the page so that you are gripping the sheet between your index finger and thumb. In this fashion you can move the page upward so that you are always on a comfortable writing level. When the last line is finished it will be a simple matter to flip to the next page.

For the dictating machine operator—list your enclosures After you finish typing a letter, do you have to waste time going back to the beginning to check on the enclosures? Or perhaps you rely on your memory and later find you have forgotten something? Get in the habit of noting enclosures on a scratch pad as you listen to the beginning of each letter. Then when you have finished typing, consult your notes, make the proper enclosures, and go on to the next letter.

Listen before you start to type Are there quite a few corrections marked on your dictating machine tape? Did your employer forget to mark off the length of his letters? Either of these signs should tip you off to listen first. In this fashion you can take notes regarding changes, judge the length of letters, and avoid having to retype.

Use a rough draft to become familiar with a new dictator This tip is for the girl who uses a dictating machine. Until you get used to the dictator's voice and vocabulary, try making a rough draft of your letters first. In the long run this will save time, because you won't have to retype misunderstood letters. It also means less erasing and neater work. Of course after one or two disks you should be able to discard this method.

Keep an extra notebook and pencils in your employer's office You are in your employer's office on a routine matter and he suddenly asks you to take a note to Mr. Landon while it is on his mind. Do you have to rush back to your desk, find your notebook, grab some pencils (hoping they're sharp), and run back to the office? Or do you keep an extra book and sharpened pencils in your employer's office so you are prepared for these emergencies?

Get rid of routine dictation Is your employer constantly dictating the same answers to routine inquiries? See if he will let you take this task off his hands. You can easily draft replies for his signature. His time is saved and so is yours; you no longer have to take down those extra notes.

For the girl with more than one boss—keep separate notebooks When you have more than one boss it is best to keep a separate notebook for each dictator. When you have to find a letter in a hurry it is much easier to go through ten pages of notes representing one man's dictation than to go through forty pages representing the work of three or four dictators. Or, mark each page with the dictator's initials. This, at least, provides you with some means of identification.

Transcribe your notes in less time Keep your shorthand notebook standing securely while you transcribe. Take a six-inch piece of string, and tie a button on each end, and set your opened notebook between the buttons.

A piece of ribbon and two brass military buttons make an attractive as well as practical gimmick.

Set aside some time for transcription Pick a time during the day for transcribing when you are least likely to be interrupted (just as your employer should do for dictation). Time is always wasted when you have to stop work and then pick it up again. Of course, you can never be entirely free from interruptions, but you can choose an hour when they will be minimal.

Find telegrams faster Do you waste time leafing through all your notes to locate one or two telegrams that have to go out right away? Fold the pages containing telegrams diagonally across the book; they will extend beyond the cover and you will be able to locate them at a glance.

You might like this system better. When you are taking notes on a telegram, write them diagonally across the page. Then you can flip through your notes and quickly spot the telegram.

Date correspondence as soon as it arrives When a letter arrives at your office, write the date on the first page. Don't trust your memory. If the letter concerns a claim or suit against your company, date of arrival could be an important factor. Even with ordinary correspondence questions often arise about the date of arrival. If your office receives a great deal of incoming correspondence, you might consider purchasing a date stamp machine. There are some on the market that stamp the date and time of arrival simultaneously.

Handling incoming mail efficiently Sort the unopened mail according to urgency or importance—telegrams, special deliveries, air mails, first class letters, and the like.

Now check for enclosures as you open each envelope (sometimes a letter will mention an enclosure when one hasn't been included). An automatic letter opener can save time, if you have much correspondence. Keep all envelopes until you are sure every letter has the sender's address, and enclosures are all accounted for.

Instead of just taking the mail and putting it on your employer's desk, take a few more minutes to see if he will need material from the files to aid in his replies. You can usually tell from the letter just which files are necessary. If you don't pull them now, you will only be interrupted later. By anticipating the needs of your busy executive, you save time for both him and you.

Find letters faster with a daily correspondence guide   It is important that you keep a record of any incoming mail you send to another office or person for action. Otherwise, you won't be able to follow up properly or you may lose track of important letters that should have been returned to you.

For each letter you refer elsewhere, record the following in a loose-leaf book:
- date of the communication
- name of the sender
- subject
- to whom you sent the material
- action that should be taken
- your follow-up date, if any

The illustration below shows what typical entries would look like:

		DAILY MAIL RECORD		
Date	Description	To Whom Sent	Action to be taken	Follow-up
7/6	Allen, June Production Report, 7/4	C.R. Cannon	Read & Return	7/11
7/6	Jones (Amalgamated Corp.) request for copy of "Non-Destructive Testing," 7/5	Wright	Reply	
7/6	J.F. Billings & Son, Annual Report	Library	File	
7/6	Lester Township High request for tour of plant 7/5	L. Lucas	Reply	7/10

A short cut for stamping envelopes   Spread the envelopes across the table or desk so that the place for the stamps is visible on each one. Using a strip of stamps, moisten the backs of a few and hold them in your right hand. Press the first one against the top envelope, and as the stamp sticks, hold it in place with your left thumb and tear off the rest of the strip with your right hand. Continue this process with the rest of the envelopes.

A quick way to seal envelopes   To seal a stack of envelopes, place them with the address side down and the flaps open so that they are spread, fan-like, across the top of your desk. Use a sponge applicator, and, with a back-and-forth motion, moisten each flap with one stroke. Starting with the envelope on top, use one hand to seal and the other to push the envelope aside while you seal the next one.

Avoid rushing with a planned mail schedule At the end of each day do you face a rush job at the mailing table? Arrange your daily schedule so that you have certain periods in which to prepare the mail. The best times are those periods right before the post office pickups. Then the few letters remaining at closing time can be prepared in a matter of minutes.

Save time on routine mailings Suppose that each week you have to mail material to the same thirty salesmen. To save time in this operation, follow these three steps:

1. Type stencils of their addresses, listing ten on a page—you will have three stencils, of course.
2. Make fifty-two copies from each stencil, using gummed-back paper.
3. Cut the sheets into individual labels and affix to envelopes.

In three simple operations you will have prepared a supply of envelopes for mailings for an entire year.

Simplify inter-office correspondence with subject headings This saves a great deal of time when you are trying to locate follow-ups and files. Your company may already have this procedure. If it doesn't, you may suggest it. Here is how it works.

Everyone who writes a memo puts a subject heading at the top to indicate the contents. If they are replying to a memo, this should also be noted. Thus the beginning of a memo might look like this:

    TO: L.B. Hall
    FR: R.J. Willis
    RE: Roland Contract (Reply your memo 9/11)

Simplify your letter writing Keep a special binder to contain extra copies of the different kinds of letters you type. (Make these extra copies in addition to the usual carbons you type for filing purposes.) On each copy, mark the margins and the spacing and centering measurements you used. This saves time when you are planning the format for similar letters. It will also familiarize you with your employer's style of letter writing so that you can draft some of his correspondence for him.

When you work for more than one executive If you type letters for more than one man, make out a list of each executive's preferences concerning spacing, style of letterhead, signature, and so on. By making such a list, you not only save time by not having to ask, but you give each employer what amounts to your individual attention.

A quick way to handle unanswered mail   When you have to send a follow-up to a letter that hasn't been answered, don't write a new letter restating the request. Simply send a copy of your first letter along with a form letter stating that this is a second request for a reply.

Here is how you can hurry slow responses   Some companies are notoriously slow in replying to correspondence. This can mean time-consuming follow-up. When you know a certain company is slow in responding, try enclosing a *stamped* return envelope when you write. This often draws a reply when the type of envelope that is imprinted for postage-free return won't.

Let post cards save you time   Form postal cards can be used for much of your routine correspondence such as orders, advertising, and the like. Not only do these cards save you the time and effort involved in writing letters, but the probability of quicker replies is increased. The double postal cards that have one half imprinted with your return address are almost certain to bring an immediate reply.

Out-of-date mailing lists waste your time   Boxes, binders, rollers, and the like will help you keep your mailing lists up to date. It is up to you to decide which system is best for your office. If you have a list that frequently changes, you need a file box where every person on your list is indexed on a separate card. This means you can make adjustments simply by adding or removing cards. Should you have a list that remains constant, you can use a loose-leaf binder and list the names down each page.

You should check your mailing list from time to time to see that business titles or divisions have not been changed. Keep an eye on business cards and letterheads to be sure you have the latest information. It is also a good idea to date any changes you make on your list.

A well-planned stationery drawer can save time   To save time in typing correspondence, place the stationery in the slanting compartments of your drawer in the same order as you would make up a carbon pack. Thus you would put letterheads in the first section, carbon paper in the second, second-sheet typing paper in the third and so on according to the number and kinds of copies you usually make.

Materials you should have on hand   Here are five areas where you can save time by keeping your supplies up to date.

1. *Keep copies of all printed forms in your file.* Most companies utilize a certain amount of printed forms, depending upon their size and the kind of business they conduct. Although you probably don't use all the forms that your company stocks, it is a good idea for you to keep a few copies of each type. Then when an emergency occurs you won't have to waste time locating the proper form.

2. *Keep a box of greeting cards in your desk.* You are ready for all occasions, including birthdays, anniversaries, promotions, and the like when you have a supply of greeting cards in your desk drawer. No more time wasted running down to the stationery store, and your employer will appreciate the convenience of having a selection right in the office.

3. *It's a good idea to keep some plain paper handy, too.* This is plain stationery without a company letterhead. There may be some occasion—for example, a letter of sympathy—for which your employer would want to use plain paper. Here again you can avoid last minute rushing by keeping a supply in your desk.

4. *Save time with stamps and stickers.* There are several types of stamps and stickers on the market today. Check them all and then decide which are best suited to your office. You will be surprised at the time you can save when you don't have to write the same information over and over.

5. *Keep your ink pad ready for use.* Turn your ink pad upside down when you are not using it. The ink runs to the top and keeps the pad ready for use with your rubber stamp whenever needed.

Save typing time with full block style   The full block style letter with open punctuation is a real time saver for the busy secretary. Check the example on page 23.

Using forms as office streamliners   Do you type the same information in triplicate each week? Reports that are typed in the same manner week after week can probably be more economically presented on a form, and in less time, too. Think of the time you save when all you have to do is type in information in its proper place on the form.

It will be up to you to check on your work and decide whether a form is necessary. If you are in a large concern, you may already have a separate department, called the Forms Control Department or some similar name. In any case, take your suggestions to your employer first and obtain his approval. Then you can contact Forms Control or go ahead on your own.

Parker Publishing Company

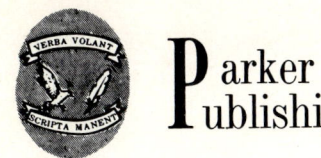

August 19, 19--

Miss Joan R. Larson
The Secretaries' School
1707 Maple Street
Whitestone, Vermont

Dear Miss Larson:

You have asked how the secretary can save time in typing correspondence. One definite way is to adopt the full block style. This letter is an example of the full block style.

First of all, there are no indentations. Everything begins at the extreme left margin, including the date and complimentary close. This eliminates the time usually taken to clear the tabulating mechanism and set up new stops. It also cancels the extra motion of hitting the tab key at the beginning of each paragraph.

You will note that the dictator's initials are not included in the identification line. We have dropped this practice since the man's name is already typed in the signature.

The secretary with a heavy load of correspondence will find this style a definite asset in getting the work out quickly and neatly.

Sincerely,

Jeanette Stuart
Correspondence Chief

cw

Working with the Forms Control Department The Forms Control Department (or whatever it's called in your company) is comprised of experts who have made a thorough study of forms and their uses and can cut down waste and operating costs in many areas. Their purpose is to provide efficient forms, so don't be afraid to take your ideas to them. Whether you're suggesting a new form or have an idea about revising an old one, let them make a study of the situation. It is what they are paid to do.

3

Faster Filing and Finding Tips

HOW MUCH TIME DO YOU WASTE LOOKING FOR "LOST files"? Do you ever lose track of appointments or forget about material requiring follow-up? This section is full of ideas on how to keep papers at the tips of your fingers, and how to make sure every appointment and promise your executive makes is kept. These tips will make your job easier and earn you a reputation for dependability.

Finding current files faster Is your desk cluttered with papers that can't be filed because they might be called for at any moment? Try keeping a special cabinet for current files right next to your desk. Sort papers daily into the categories you use and place them out of sight in handy folders. Not only will your desk look neater, but you will actually be able to find the material faster when your employer asks for it.

If your employer is open to time-saving suggestions, consider asking him to keep a file drawer in his desk for his most current projects. This will save his time and yours. As he completes a project he can give the material to you to put in the permanent files.

- *caution* A current file system does more harm than good if you don't weed it out regularly. Set a definite time limit for material to be filed there. On each paper filed, note the date when it is to be transferred to the permanent file. Then be sure to remove old material as you use the file each day.

An easy way to find files—use colored labels The use of tabs of different colors can be a real time saver. You can distinguish between categories in your files at a glance. Let's say that in your office you keep records for five years; you could easily and quickly distinguish each year's files by using a different color for each year.

Of more frequent help would be a color coding for your alphabetical files. Use a different color tab or label for each letter of the alphabet. This saves time, and it also prevents misfiling, which can be a problem if several people are using the same files.

Labels should be easy to read If you have trouble finding or filing papers, the fault may not be with the system you are using; it may simply be that your labels are hard to read. Neat and legible identification on file guides and folders can make an enormous difference in the speed and accuracy of your filing, and can make it easier on your eyes as well.

First of all, always type tabs or labels; hand-written tabs are almost invariably more difficult to read, and are more subject to smudging.

Be uniform in making labels. For example:

- Decide whether you will begin typing a caption two or three spaces from the left margin of the label, and always do it that way. Captions will then line up properly in the file drawers; your eye can move in a straight line along them.
- Type captions in the same style. Lower case is probably best because solid capital letters are somewhat harder to read.
- Type close to the top of labels so that captions don't get covered up.

"Out" folders save time and work When you remove a folder from the files you probably replace it with an "out" card or slip, telling what folder is missing and who has it. This is an almost essential procedure when several people use the same files. But you probably find that while a folder is out of the files, material comes in that should be filed in it.

Rather than let such papers pile up on your desk waiting for the folder to come back, try this idea. Instead of using a card or slip to indicate that a folder is out of the files, use a folder. Put the usual information on the outside—the title or subject of the folder removed, date of removal, name and department of person using it, and the date on which it should be returned. Inside the folder put the material that comes in while the original folder is out.

When the original folder is returned, just transfer the new material to it. The "out" folder can be used over and over again (you may need several handy if your files are extensive).

This system keeps your desk neater and your files up to date, and it saves papers from getting lost or mangled before they can be properly filed.

- *tip* Try using a special color tab to identify "out" folders. You can instantly find the proper place for the original folder when it returns.

Finding large-size papers faster When filing large-size papers (special reports, accounting sheets, charts, and the like) don't fold them so that the information is on the inside. Think of all the time you waste pulling out and opening several sheets before you find the one you want. Instead, fold the papers so that the written material is on the outside. Besides saving your valuable time, this trick saves the papers from abuse of constant handling.

A new way to staple papers for filing You probably staple papers together at the top left corner. When stapled papers are filed, therefore, the staple is at the bottom of the file drawer, and it is easy to file other papers between the stapled sheets by mistake. To avoid this, staple papers at the top right corner. You will be able to turn the top sheet over just as easily. The stapled corner will now be at the top in the file drawer, so that other papers can't get in between.

Stay ahead of alphabetical sorting The job of arranging a large batch of papers in alphabetical order can be a headache. Fortunately, there are ways to simplify the task.

If part of your job is the making of an alphabetical list or report at the end of the month, or week, it's possible that you are doing it the hard way. Let's say that at the end of each month your executive needs a tally, in alphabetical order, of shipments that have gone out to dealers. You receive copies of shipping papers each day, and from these papers you compile your list at the end of the month. If you wait until the last minute to alphabetize, you may well be turning a small task into a difficult one. It will be much easier if you have a folder set up for each dealer (or one for each letter of the alphabet, if you have random names). Each day, as shipping papers come in, file them away properly in the appropriate folders. At the end of the month your alphabetizing will already be done.

When you have a large sorting job, alphabetize in stages If you have two or three hundred sheets to put into alphabetical order, don't try to alphabetize strictly right away. Instead, begin by dividing the material into four main groups: A to F, G to L, M to R, and S to Z. You will handle each sheet more than once before you are finished, but you will still find that this method saves time and is more accurate and less fatiguing than trying to do it all at once.

Save time by filing backwards in loose-leaf binders How much time have you wasted thumbing through loose-leaf sheets to get to the current page? If you want to save time, try filing backwards.

Arrange the binder so that you add sheets in the front instead of in the back. You will find that not only will you save time, but the pages will be neater looking since you won't be handling all of them every time you want the most recent sheet.

Preserve your neat files—compile a filing guide Have you ever returned from a vacation or sick leave to find your files in shambles because no one else could find things, or knew how to put them back? Or perhaps you have come in the morning to find that your boss was working late the night before and needed some files that he didn't know where to find. Probably he rummaged around until he found them and then left the resulting mess for you to clean up.

All of this extra work and lost time could have been avoided if you had a filing guide showing just where everything is filed and how it is filed. The easiest way to compile the guide is in three parts. *Section One* explains the rules governing the various filing systems in your office. This includes alphabetical filing, numerical filing, filing by date, procedure for removing material from file and procedure for replacing files. It also covers the files kept in other offices in your company. This means that no one will waste time going through your files looking for information that someone else has.

A typical excerpt from Section One would read:

Customer File	Folders are filed alphabetically by Company Name with cross index for important individual names.	
	Location	Area 2
	Out Procedure . .	Insert OUT folder after noting subject of material removed, your name, department and date on face of folder.
	In Procedure . .	Remove OUT folder and mark it RETURNED, date and initial. Place material back in–file. Put OUT folder in box on top of file.
Claim File	Folders filed alphabetically by claimant.	
	Location	Area 3
	Out Procedure . .	All folders must be signed out with Miss Hayes in Area 3.

Faster Filing and Finding Tips • 29

	In Procedure . . Folders to be refiled are left in Claim File basket on Miss Hayes' desk. Do not return folder directly to file.
Employee File	Folders filed alphabetically by employee's last name.
	Location . . . . Area 5
	Out Procedure . . Strictly Personal File—Must clear with Mr. Adams before anyone can see file.
	In Procedure . . Return to Mr. Adams' secretary.

Section Two is an alphabetical listing of all material the company keeps on file, cross referenced where necessary. Each listing should be followed by an entry stating where the material is located and the name of the file. You then refer to Section One to find out the method of filing and the procedure for taking material out.

A typical entry in Section Two would read:

Addresses, Employee...............	Area 5
	Employee File (Strictly Personal—see Section One)
Buyers	Area 2
	Customer File
Claims	Area 3
	Claims File

Section Three contains floor maps showing where files are located. The map of each floor should look something like this:

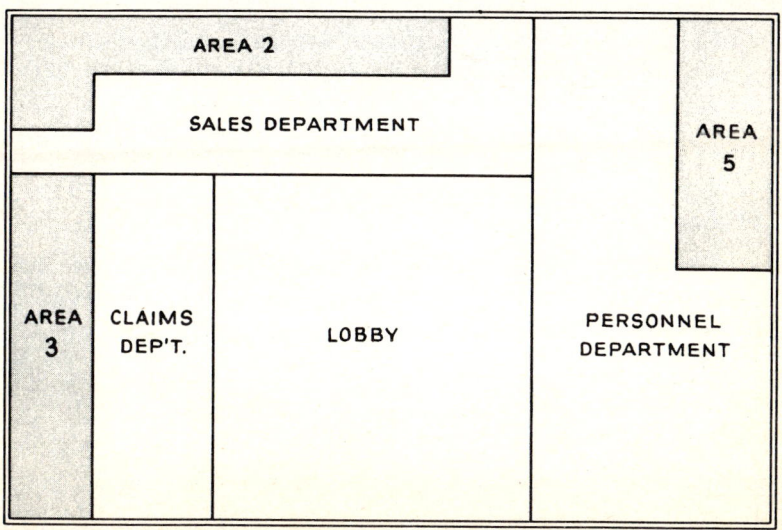

FIRST FLOOR

Every secretary needs a follow-up system You can't rely on your memory to accomplish everything at the proper time—and a missed deadline or appointment, or a reply that was never made to an important customer, can have disastrous consequences.

These are typical matters that must be followed up:

1. Correspondence whose reply must await the gathering of information, or a decision or action
2. Orders specifying future delivery dates
3. Matters referred to other executives or departments for information or advice
4. Matters requiring attention at regular intervals: salary consideration, company reports, contract renewals and the like.

There will also be many miscellaneous promises made by either you or your executive which must be followed up, too.

There is no one method of handling a follow-up system. Your office may do so much following up on correspondence and orders that it requires a filing system designed just for follow-up work. The manufacturers of filing equipment can provide as elaborate a system as you need, if that is your situation. However, the system we describe below is adequate for most offices, and it involves no extra expense, apart from the cost of the folders used.

Note that in the system we recommend, no original papers go in the follow-up file; it contains only copies of material to be followed up, or notations of what must be done. The originals go in the regular files, where they can always be found without a double search.

Setting up the file The file is arranged so that the folder in the front of the file drawer each morning is the one containing material that needs handling that day.

To set up the file, you need 44 folders, labeled as follows:

31 folders numbered from 1 to 31, for days of the month
12 folders labeled for months of the year
 1 folder labeled "Future Years"

Assume for the moment that you are setting up your file on the first day of a month. In the front of the file drawer, in order, put the numbered folders, representing the days of the current month. Behind them, beginning with the *forthcoming* month, place the monthly folders, with the current month *last* (ready to start collecting for the same month next year). At the rear goes the folder for future years.

Operating the file The follow-up file (also called a "tickler file") is very simple to use, and is worth its weight in gold. All it requires from you is *regular* use.

What you put into the file. You must put into the file a reminder for each matter that will need future attention. This works as follows:

• Incoming correspondence: For each piece of incoming correspondence that requires follow-up, place a memo in the follow-up file. File the letter itself in the regular files.

• Outgoing correspondence: When you type up a letter that will need following up, make a copy for the follow-up file.

• Other items: For something that can be duplicated on a machine, make a copy for the follow-up file. If it cannot be copied, put a memo into the follow-up file instead.

Mark a follow-up date on each paper you place in the tickler file. If the follow-up date on an item is a month or less away, place the item in the appropriate numbered folder. Less pressing items go in the folder for the month in which their follow-up date falls, or into the "Future Years" folder, if that is called for.

Consult the tickler daily. Each morning, take out the material from the folder for that day, and place the empty folder in order behind the folder for the next month. In this way the daily folders gradually shift from the current month to the forthcoming month.

The illustration shows how the file would look on the morning of the 15th day of a month. Notice that folders representing non-working days are reversed to reduce the chance of misfiling.

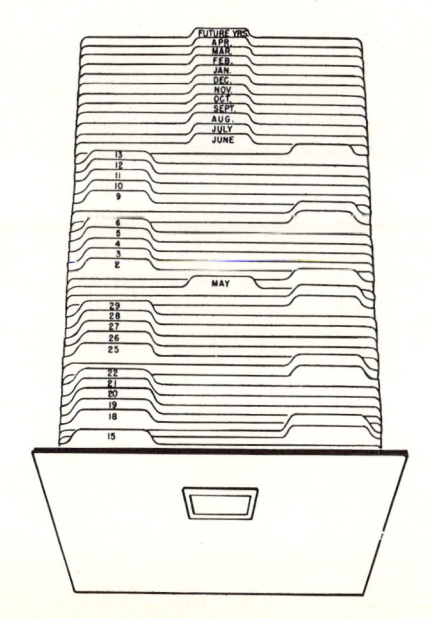

Folder Arrangement for Follow-up File

You will often find that items in the follow-up file have already been taken care of. In that case just throw away the memo or copy that was to serve as a reminder. If a matter has an indefinite follow-up date, or you cannot handle it on the day you were supposed to, mark it with a new date and file it in the appropriate folder.

Check at the beginning of each month. On the first day of each month, remove the material from that month's folder and place the folder behind the other monthly folders. File the material in the proper daily folders, according to follow-up date (many of these folders will already hold material you have filed in them on a day-by-day basis over the preceding 31 days).

Check when a new year begins. Don't forget to look in the "Future Years" folder the first working day of each year.

A follow-up file on a smaller scale Perhaps your office does not have a great amount of correspondence requiring follow-up. In this case a single follow-up folder may do the trick. Simply mark all carbons and memos with the follow-up date and file them chronologically (by follow-up date) in the folder. On the top you should have those marked for the earliest follow-up. Each day check the folder for things that should be done that day.

You can also use a card file as a tickler file. It would be set up just as the folders are, with reminders typed on cards instead of placed in folders. The disadvantage is that it means an extra file, because carbons of outgoing letters are usually used as reminders, and they are placed in a folder. Most secretaries find it less confusing to use folders for their tickler file.

Streamlining your files Cluttered files mean wasted time when you have to locate something in a hurry. Don't let this happen in your office. Here are some suggestions for low cost streamlining.

Hanging folders and hanging pockets are streamliners. You may find hanging folders and hanging pockets a help in solving space problems. These hang on a frame that fits into the file drawer. The hanging folder can save space because it serves as a guide, a folder and a separator all in one. But if too many of them are used in a single file drawer, the space-saving feature is lost, because a hanging folder actually takes up more space than a standard folder. Even so, hanging folders will help save time by making papers easier to find and remove, and by keeping papers from getting lost in the bottom of the file drawer.

You may find that hanging pockets are a better space-saving device than hanging folders. You need fewer of them in a drawer, so they add less bulk. Pockets expand, so that several ordinary folders can be put into them. They are especially useful when your files are strictly alphabetical or numerical; each pocket can be labeled for a group of letters or numbers (A-F, for example, or 101-120) for separation and easy reference.

Using portable drawer dividing units. A portable drawer divider is another device to eliminate bulky follow blocks. The divider is a lightweight metal "skeleton" easily inserted into a drawer; it separates and supports file folders, holding them upright.

This dividing unit serves other purposes, too. It can be inserted into a desk drawer to hold miscellaneous papers, brochures, stationery and other supplies. It can be used on the desk-top, to hold letters or magazines. It is adjustable, so that sections can be expanded or narrowed, as needed.

Don't keep old magazines in the files. Magazines, brochures and other bulky items of a periodical nature shouldn't be allowed to crowd more important material out of the files. Try to keep current issues on a shelf or table where they are accessible (no one will ever see them if they are buried in the files). Older issues should either be thrown out, or, if they must be kept as reference material, stored in a place other than the files.

Sometimes, however, you must keep pamphlets or brochures in the files.

Here are two ways to save space when you are filing such material:

1. Narrow pamphlets and brochures, only a fraction of the size of the folder that holds them, should be stacked in double or triple rows, lengthwise, within the folder.

2. Printed matter that is clipped or bound on one edge should be equalized by alternating the papers within the folder; with half of the bulky edges to the right side of the folder and half to the left.

Eliminate duplications from your files. An obvious way to keep your files slim is to prevent duplicate filing. Duplications often occur in the following areas:

    1. carbon copies of memos and letters
    2. galleys, page proofs, and paste-ups
    3. reprints of published letters and reports
    4. identical copies of published brochures

Like many secretaries, you may have a habit of making two or three carbons of each letter or report you type, "just in case." But unless your executive really needs those extra copies for some special purpose, you may be stuffing your files with unnecessary paper. Try making as few copies as necessary on every typing job—a duplicating machine can provide more copies if there is an unexpected need for them.

Unless you plan to distribute additional copies of brochures or reports, the filing of identical copies of printed matter is unnecessary. Many secretaries retain three copies of this type of material and send the remaining copies to storage spaces located in a remote part of the building.

Use thinner backings for clippings and photos. The kind of cardboard that is often used as backing for photographs and clippings that will be filed is quite thick. For less bulk and better protection, try using envelopes of celluloid. Or, if this would be too costly, substitute Manila tag for the cardboard; it is strong, yet thinner than cardboard.

Put those little-used materials in storage. Don't clutter up your everyday file with papers that are only needed once or twice a year. See if your company has an area for storage and then arrange to have those seldom used files moved there. You can even obtain transfer files, which are regulation size file drawers made of cardboard and enclosed in cardboard casings. There is ample room to label each drawer.

If there is no storage room available try putting the lesser used files in the top and bottom drawers of your file cabinet. In this fashion you keep your daily files within easy reach in the middle drawers.

Weed out disposable papers daily. One of your jobs is to carry out your company's records retention and disposal program. To simplify this duty, use a colored pencil to mark on each paper as you get it what its throw-out date is. This makes the date easy to spot as you are going through the files.

Then, as you file each day, be on the lookout for papers on which the throw-out date has come due; pull these papers and discard them. If you have any question, consult your executive before you throw a paper out.

With this system, you keep your files clean each day automatically. Your files never get a chance to get clogged with papers that should have been cleaned out.

- **caution** If your company doesn't have a records retention and disposal program, don't take it upon yourself to set one up. There are many factors to consider, including legal ones, in deciding how long to keep business papers.

Office calendars save you time, promote efficiency Do you have to sort through scraps of paper to make sure you haven't forgotten an appointment or a special job your employer wants completed? Perhaps you have even scheduled two appointments for the same time because you forgot to keep a proper record. If you have had any of these problems it is time you started keeping office calendars. They will tell you at a glance just what is on the agenda for today, tomorrow and next month. By working them out with your executive you avoid all confusion and save time.

Your executive's yearly calendar. There are many kinds of yearly calendars available to the executive. The design and scope of the calendar will vary with the manufacturer. Some yearly calendars are highly specialized, while others can be used by any type of office.

The yearbook type calendar that closes and can be put away in a desk drawer has an advantage over the standard desk calendar pad. Since these calendars often contain appointments and other information that your employer considers confidential, he will not want to leave it open on his desk when callers are present. He cannot, however, pointedly remove a standard type calendar from under a visitor's nose, but he can casually close a yearbook and put it aside under the guise of straightening up his desk.

An executive's calendar should have sufficient space for entering all his appointments including both the other party, his name, and his company and for noting important occasions that affect his schedule.

Should your employer be an attorney, controller, or accountant he will need a larger type yearbook which is generally known as a diary. There is more space in these calendars so that callers, appointments, matters requiring special attention, and the like can be recorded. Also you have room to keep a record of work that has been completed and the amount of time spent doing it.

Some of the typical entries your executive's yearly calendar might include are notations of his monthly board meetings, special holidays, family anniversaries, annual conventions, client or departmental meetings. (A complete list of recurring items may be found on page 38.) You do not enter in your executive's calendar any items that are merely reminders to you, such as the date certain checks have to be sent out.

Be sure to consult your executive's calendar at the end of the day to see if he has entered any appointments that he forgot to tell you about. This small step can save much confusion.

A calendar for you. You need a reminder system, too. You can use a standard desk calendar pad or a yearbook for your calendar. There should be 15-minute or 30-minute divisions so you can note each day's events in detail. Your calendar will have notations of all of your employer's activities and items which you have to notify him about, plus all your own activities for the day.

You can check it quickly when he asks about something or you are on the telephone. If there is a special trip or similar event which requires advance preparation, be sure to make a notation in your calendar in advance of the actual date, so you have time.

Keeping a monthly calendar. Many executives like to be able to

APPOINTMENTS

Nov. 15 Mon.		-	
		- 12:00 Noon	-Preliminary Meetg. - New York Printers' Society
		- 3:00 P.M.	- Clarion Bd. Meetg.
"	16 Tue.	- 1:30 P.M.	- Architecture Forum
"	17 Wed.	- 5:30 P.M.	- United Char. - Parlor B - New York Athletic Club
"	18 Thu.	- 6:00 P.M.	- Apex Club-Albany Pub. Expenditure Coun. -WTH
"	18 Thu.	- 6:30 P.M.	-Executive Dinner - Astor Hotel
"	19 Fri.	- 12:15 P.M.	- Amer. Trade Assn.
		- 6: ? P.M.	- New York Engrg. Soc. Panel
Nov. 22 Mon.		-	
"	23 Tue.	- 1:30 P.M.	- Architecture Forum
"	24 Wed.	-	- Michaelson
"	25 Thu.	-	- Thanksgiving
"	26 Fri.	- Evening	- Clarion Dance - Princeton Inn
Nov. 29 Mon.		-	
		-	- Check to S. Shirer
"	30 Tue.	- 1:30 P.M.	- Architecture Forum
Dec. 1 Wed.		-	- Michaelson
"	2 Thu.	-	- Talk at Albany - Wm. Lennan
"	3 Fri.	-	-
Dec. 6 Mon.		-	
"	7 Tue.	- 1:30	- Architecture Forum
		- 6:00 P.M.	- Service Club - Statler Hotel
"	8 Wed.	-	- Michaelson
"	9 Thu.	-	-
"	10 Fri.	- 10:00 A.M.	- ATCC Meeting - Hotel New Yorker

Four-Week Schedule

see coming engagements at a glance. A monthly calendar will do the trick. You may have a commercial calendar—from a customer, perhaps—that is large enough and has sufficient room to make daily entries. Or you can buy calendars for this purpose.

Keeping a four-week schedule. In addition to appointments, a four-week schedule lists holidays, evening social functions, and things to be done. Since it is a running schedule, it must be typed each week in order to be kept up to date. If your employer keeps this schedule on his desk you may consider mounting it on a piece of cardboard to make handling easier. The four-week schedule is most helpful when your boss plans to be away from the office for a week or more. His first step is usually a quick check of scheduled activities for the period he intends to be absent. From there on he can plan his trip without worrying about having forgotten something important. See an illustration of the four-week schedule on page 36.

Keeping a daily schedule. Perhaps the most important and useful reminder of all is a detailed daily schedule for your executive, telling him exactly what he has scheduled for the day.

Place on his desk each morning a typed schedule of his appointments, showing the name of each caller, the time he is expected, his affiliation, purpose of the call, and any additional information you consider pertinent. You can use 6 x 9 inch memorandum paper; he can easily slip this into his pocket if he has to go out.

A pocket memo is also valuable. If your executive does much of his work outside the office, a pocket memo calendar book will prevent him from making conflicting commitments while he is away from his desk. The pocket memo briefly lists yearly events and future appointments that would conflict with appointments your employer himself might make. In the memo book your employer records any new appointments

---

APPOINTMENTS FOR WEDNESDAY, JULY 17

10:30 A.M.	Appointment with Mr. Allen - discuss building contract.
11:00	Call George Bailey - see if field reports are in.
12:00	Lunch with Herb Anderson - Ad Men's Club
1:00 P.M.	Meeting with Department Heads - discuss Costello account
3:30	Meet Jim West at Benton Building

Daily Schedule

he has made. Each time he returns to the office, ask if you may check the memo book to see if any new appointments were made.

Preparing calendars is easier when you use a tickler card file The method of setting up a tickler card file is explained on page 30. Such a file can save you time when many items on a calendar require repeated action. For example, instead of making fifty-two notations on your calendar of some weekly duty, make out one card, which you can move ahead each week. A card has more space for complete information than a calendar does, too.

- *caution* Don't use a card file to note appointments. All engagements and appointments are entered on the calendar; otherwise, whenever you need to make a new appointment for your executive you would have to look not only at the calendar but also at the tickler file. With all engagements and appointments entered on the calendar, you do not keep someone waiting while you go through the tickler cards.

Each morning refer to your calendar and then your tickler file. In this way you will be aware of all key entries on the calendar and any details recorded in the tickler file. Keep a list of events that recur each year. Early in October enter all the recurring items for the forthcoming year in the calendar for the next year. If your employer makes important engagements far in advance you may have to make up the yearly calendars even earlier. Work from the list of recurring events when preparing your calendar. The dates of the events often change and thus last year's calendar is not applicable. For example, if conferences are held on the first Monday of every month, the actual dates of these conferences will vary from year to year. And if you rely on last year's calendar dates you might schedule certain business activities for a Sunday or a holiday.

Here is a check list for recurring items that a secretary usually enters on the calendars for each year. Everyone's situation is different, so you'll want to add some or take some off.

Check List of Recurring Items

Family Dates
  Anniversaries
  Birthdays (members of your executive's family and any other birthdays he may want to remember)
  Father's Day
  Mother's Day

Holidays
  Christmas. (As the purpose of this item is to bring up the gift and card lists, the entry date depends on the shopping conditions in your locality and on the number of presents on your employer's list. Six weeks is the average time required.)

Easter
Election Day
New Year's Day
Religious Holidays
Thanksgiving
Valentine's Day
Meetings
Board meetings (company and outside directorates)
Club meetings
Committee meetings (company and outside activities)
Conventions
Stockholders' annual meeting
Payment Dates
Contributions, under pledges or otherwise, to religious and charitable organizations. If weekly, enter each Friday as the date on which to draw the check.
Insurance premium due dates
Interest on notes payable and maturity dates of notes. Enter notation about a week before due dates. Your employer's funds might be low or he might want to negotiate a renewal.
Interest on notes reecivable and maturity dates of notes. If it is necessary to send a reminder to a debtor, enter ten days before the due date.
Periodic payments, such as salaries to servants, allowance to children, tuition payments, and the like. If the date the check should be sent falls on a day that the office is closed, enter it on preceding day.
Renewal Dates
Automobile license
Hunting and fishing license
Dog or cat license
Subscriptions to periodicals
Tax Dates
Federal taxes. Enter tax items on your calendar in advance of the due dates to allow ample time for preparation of returns.
State and local taxes

4

The Telephone as a Time Saver

ARE YOU GETTING THE MOST OUT OF YOUR OFFICE telephone? It should be saving you time, but many secretaries fail to use it to full advantage. Try the following tips to increase your telephone efficiency.

Save time by making calls successively You make several telephone calls in the course of your normal business day. Ordinarily you would have to interrupt your work each time one of these calls had to be placed. Each interruption means time wasted in putting a project down and having to pick it up again. Why not save time by placing your calls successively? Gather the information necessary for each call and then place them one after the other. If possible, set aside a certain time each day for this work.

Keep a list of numbers you call often Your employer calls certain people more often than others. Are you continually looking up the same numbers day after day? If this is the case then you are wasting valuable time. Make a list of the telephone numbers and extensions most frequently called and then find a convenient place to keep it. You might tape it to the pull-out shelf in your desk.

Try keeping a telephone and address book This would include the names and addresses, as well as telephone numbers, of all your executive's business associates. Sometimes an associate will also be a personal friend of your employer. When this is the case include his home telephone number in your book.

Also included on this list might be the telephone numbers for your employer's children's schools, stores where he keeps charge accounts, the garage where he services his car, his wife's beauty parlor, and so on. You will be surprised at how much time you can save when you have this information at your fingertips.

- **note** Don't forget to include the code numbers for dialing exchanges that are not in your immediate area.

Of course you should always keep a local telephone directory by your desk. There will be instances where you will need some information that is not in your office book. Your office visitors will appreciate having it on hand, too.

Speed your long distance calls   First mark off all the long distance numbers on your telephone list by placing a check in the margin. Then locate a time chart and note the differences in time between the other cities and your own.

When your employer makes frequent long distance calls you might find it helpful to have pertinent business information kept with the appropriate telephone numbers.

For complete information you can also list who can be reached on a station-to-station call and who needs a person-to-person connection.

With this information on hand, long distance calls should not take much longer than your regular calls. A sample page from your telephone book will look something like this:

Name & Title	Address	Dial Code	Business Phone	Home Phone	Time Differential
Andrews, John P. Vice President, Sales	Apex Corp. 3001 Clay Ave. San Fran. California 5211	413	Jefferson 1-2299		2 hrs. earlier than Chicago (S-S)
Antoine's Jewelry	153 Jefferson Street Chi. 49, Ill.		191-4264		
Armstrong, Wm. R. Manager, Advert.	Apex Corp. 1297 Madison Ave. N.Y. N.Y. 07131	212	315-3533	567-4273	1 hr. later than Chicago (P-P in A.M., S-S in P.M.)
Arnold, Robt. S Principal	Central H.S. Lincoln Sq. Chi. 38, Ill.		191-3255		

Keep a map near your telephone Out-of-town visitors or business associates often call to find out how to get to your office. They may be coming in by plane, train, bus or automobile. With an area map on hand you can give immediate directions with a minimum loss of time.

How to keep your telephone clean Here is a quick way to get at that dirt under the dialing ring. Simply moisten a few cotton balls and place them in two or three dial holes. Dial a few times and the telephone is clean.

Identify yourself and your office when you answer the phone A man calling during business hours has a right to expect prompt service. A vague "Hello" means he has to waste your time and his own finding out if he has the right extension. When you answer the telephone simply say "Mr. Brown's office, Miss Jones speaking." Now all your caller has to do is introduce himself and state his business.

Special equipment can save time and work It's always a good idea to keep up with the new developments in the communications field. Often they turn out to be real time savers for the secretary. For instance, consider the new card-operated dial telephone. If you frequently dial the same numbers for your employer, this device can be a real time saver. The telephone numbers are coded on individual perforated cards. To place a call, merely put the card in the special slot and the number will be dialed for you automatically.

Does your executive wander through the company so that you never know where to reach him when an important call comes in? Perhaps you can use one of the new paging devices now on the market. Your executive can carry a portable receiver around in his pocket which will enable you to buzz him when he is wanted on the phone. It is also possible to obtain a walkie-talkie type with which you can actually converse with him right from your desk, even though he is on the other side of the building.

There is a paging system available now that lets your executive do his own paging on inter-office calls. When his party doesn't answer, he merely dials a special extension number which is connected to the paging system and does his own paging. This saves you the trouble of having to contact the switchboard operator or do the job yourself whenever your boss needs someone in a hurry.

5

Office Machines Can Save Work

ARE YOU DOING JOBS BY HAND THAT COULD BE COMpleted faster by machine? Office machines are designed to make your work load lighter. Find out about the new equipment that could save time on those routine chores. Here are some of the basic areas where you can start.

A word about the manufacturers The companies mentioned in this chapter are but a few of the many who make and market business machines. The Yellow Pages of your telephone directory will give you a list of manufacturers and their representatives in your area. Also, you may consult your stationer when you want information on a specific type of machine.

Dictating machines are real time savers Dictating machines save your employer's time as well as your own. The double job of taking down notes and then transcribing them is eliminated. While your employer dictates you can be accomplishing other tasks. Also, your employer can dictate at his convenience without worrying about when he can take you from other work.

Types of machines. There are a great variety of dictating machines on the market. Some use tape while others use wire, plastic belts, records, or even recording sheets the size of a normal letter. It will be up to your employer to decide which type suits his purposes.

Recording time. This varies according to the machine and the method of recording. If your employer has heavy correspondence he may prefer a tape or wire machine that records up to two or three hours of material. A man with urgent letters or very light dictation might prefer a machine utilizing ten-or-fifteen-minute belts or records.

Some of the companies producing these machines include (in alphabetical order) DeJur Grundig, Dictaphone Corporation, GBC American Corporation, IBM, Lanier Business Products, Inc., North-American Philips Co., Inc. (Norelco), and Vanguard.

New portable dictating machines. Now your employer doesn't have to do all his dictating in the office. He can dictate at home, in the car, or on a plane. As with the desk models, portable machines are available for cassettes, tape, wire, or record. Again, recording time can vary from ten minutes to three hours. These machines are small enough to fit into an attaché case, or even a suit pocket in some instances. Most have carrying cases available. A few of the manufacturers of such equipment include (in alphabetical order) DeJur Grundig (Stenorette), Dictaphone Corporation (Dictet), GBC America Corp. (Stenomaster), Lanier Business Products, Inc., Minifon Co., and Telefunken Corporation. For suppliers near you, consult the Yellow Pages of your telephone directory.

Mailing machines can speed up a tiresome chore How much time do you waste slitting envelopes every morning? And how much time is wasted stuffing envelopes and applying stamps every afternoon? If your office handles any appreciable amount of mail, your employer may be interested in the new mailing machines now on the market. They will cut this chore down to a minimum and leave you free to perform more important tasks. Here are some of the machines available:

For opening envelopes. For offices with light mail there is the hand operated envelope opener. Simply insert the envelope, push the handle, and the envelope is slit across the top. The contents are never touched, so you don't have to worry about damaging checks or statements. Actually the operation is much safer than opening by hand.

Offices with large mail volume need the high speed electric opener. Here you can stack the envelopes on the machine and they will go through automatically and stack themselves, open, on the other side.

An office with a medium amount of mail or a high amount of bulk mail can use a special model opener that not only handles regular mail but also allows you to open an envelope on three sides. This is of special concern to banks, financial and shipping concerns.

One well-known manufacturer of these machines is Pitney-Bowes, Inc., but there are several. Ask your office equipment supplier about the machines he offers.

Stamping and sealing envelopes. Most metering machines also seal envelopes. This means you stamp and seal in one operation. Some machines dispense a paper strip with a metered stamp that shows the amount of postage, while others simply stamp the envelope. Actually, the postage meter is a separate machine entirely, even though it is incorporated with your office mailing machine. You don't purchase a meter but only rent it from a manufacturer who is licensed by the Post Office Department. It is up to the manufacturer to see that the machines are used correctly. After renting the machine you take it to your post office and pay for the postage in advance. The machine is then set for whatever amount you specify. On returning to the office the meter is placed in a special section of the mailing machine and you are ready to start operation.

Machines for addressing envelopes. Do you send out large batches of mail to the same people on a regular basis? In that case you can use an automatic envelope addressing machine. You simply type a card or a stencil for each address and insert the cards with the envelopes into the machine. The cards can be used over and over, thus saving you the time-consuming job of typing envelopes every time a mailing has to go out. Manufacturers of this type of machine include Dashew Business Machines, Inc. and Elliott Industries, Inc.

Machines for inserting mail. For really large-scale operations there are machines that will collect enclosures, fold and place them in envelopes, seal the envelopes, stamp them (optional) and stack them. One machine even has a provision for affixing address labels. Manufacturers of these machines include EnMail Machine Corporation and Pitney-Bowes, Inc.

Copying machines—the quick, easy answer for extra copies How many times have you finished typing a letter or report only to find yourself one copy short? Did you start typing all over again, or did you have a copying machine on hand to give you that extra copy in a matter of seconds? In many cases it is quicker to get your copies from a copier than to type them. Most machines produce black-on-white copies that can hardly be distinguished from the originals.

Kinds of copiers There are three main processes for copying papers in the office. If you already possess one of the machines, now is the time to learn about its advantages. If you are in the market for a copier, this will give you an idea of what is available. Only a few major companies are named (usually to help identify a process), but there are many active in the field.

Photography. Of course anything photographed has to be developed, so these machines must use chemicals (but little mess is involved). Actually a copier of this nature is simply a camera and developer rolled into one. In the basic photocopy process, the material to be copied is placed on a piece of sensitized paper and put in the camera part of the machine where it is photographed. The original is returned to you while the exposed sensitized sheet is coupled with a positive sheet and placed in the developer part of the copier. A few seconds later both sheets are returned and upon separation you have your copy on the positive sheet. With some machines you can return the exposed sheet to the developer for additional copies, while with others you must start the whole process over.

The Photostat Corporation produces a copier of this type that can be used to reproduce any material that is typed, printed, or written. After one copy is made, the "negative" can be returned to the developer for additional copies.

Charles Bruning Company, Inc. has a copier that reproduces any material that is typed, written, drawn, or printed. Black-on-white or color-coded copies are also available. Bruning varies the basic photocopying process; you only need your original and one sheet of "Copyflex" paper. Once the "Copyflex" is exposed it is placed in the developer and a dry copy is returned to you in seconds.

Eastman Kodak Company manufactures the Verifax copier which will copy anything written, from ball point pen to crayon. The Verifax differs from the usual photocopying process in that you can make copies on bond-type paper, card stock, or printed office forms. You can even make offset masters or masters for whiteprint machines in about a minute.

Heat. This process literally burns an image of the original into special paper. No chemicals are used; the process is completely dry. Certain colors and inks will not be picked up. These copiers can be used to reproduce photographs, correspondence, reports, leases, deeds, and the like. The Thermo-Fax, manufactured by Minnesota Mining and Manufacturing Company, is the well-known copier in this field.

Electricity. Machines utilizing the electrostatic process use no chemicals and produce completely dry copies. You simply place the original in the machine with a sheet of the special copy paper, or in some cases regular office bond, and you have your completed copy in seconds.

The American Photocopy Equipment Company puts out a copier of this type that can be used to reproduce any material that is typed, printed, drawn, written, or photographed. Each copy made on this machine can be used to make another. Even colors will be picked up (as shades of gray). Copies are permanent and will not fade or discolor.

Savin Business Machines Corporation also makes a machine using the electrostatic process. Unlike some other machines in this field, the Savin copier will reproduce on any type of paper including letterhead, office forms, invoices, accounting forms and printed cards. It copies all colors and all writing including pencil, ball point pen, crayon, rubber stamps, symbols and line drawings. Another interesting feature of this machine is that you can make two-sided copies from two-sided originals. You can also make paper offset plates and address labels.

Heavy duty duplicators   Does your employer want one thousand copies of a special report? Or would he like an extra copy of a blueprint on the new company building? It isn't necessary to go to a printer for these tasks if you happen to have one of the new super duplicators in your company. These machines can turn out copies by the thousands and some can even provide you with plates for offset duplicating. Here are some examples of what is available. This is not a complete list; you will want further information if you need a machine of this type.

General Aniline & Film Corp., Ozalid Division. Ozalid puts out a variety of machines in the heavy duty category. They are capable of copying material up to 56 inches wide. The printing process is a simple one involving ultra-violet light. The finished copy is flat, dry (although a developer solution is used), and exactly like the original.

Charles Bruning Company, Inc. Bruning has a copier that can reproduce black-on-white, black-on-color, color-on-white, color-on-color, or multi-color prints of maps, plats, tracings, drawings, specification sheets, and the like. The printing process is the same type utilized by Ozalid and delivers up to one thousand 8½ x 11 prints per hour, depending on the model.

Copease Corporation. Copease manufactures a machine that enables you to make metal offset plates in your office and another that allows you to print from the plates. This is a simple operation taking only a few minutes. All you do is expose the plate, process it and place it on the offset duplicator. Copease duplicators take plates up to 24 by $18^{13}/_{16}$ inches.

Offset duplicating is basically a simple process. The plate bearing the information to be copied is placed in the duplicator. After passing over ink rollers, the plate transfers its image to a "blanket." The blanket is then brought into contact with the paper under pressure and the copy is formed.

Photostat Corporation. The Photostat Corporation has an offset duplicator that allows you to omit lines of copy from the bottom or either side of a systems form, so that one basic form can do many jobs. Another model serially numbers and personalizes checks in strips of five, from a direct-image plate.

Haloid Xerox Inc. The Haloid duplicators use a dry, electrical copying process which they call Xerography. Powder is attracted to the paper by an electrical charge to form an image; the paper is heated for a few seconds, which fuses the powder and forms a permanent print.

The same process is used in other Xerox duplicators to produce metal offset master plates.

Special printing jobs Do you send out post cards to customers with hand written or typed messages on the back? Why not save time and effort with a new printing device made especially for post cards. You can print your message and illustrate it at the same time. Your post cards look neater and attract more attention. Of course some of the large duplicating machines are also equipped to handle this type of printing job, but if you have a small office and are just interested in sending out post cards from time to time, a small printer is all you need.

Copying tax forms. Several manufacturers offer machines especially suited to copying tax returns and schedules. The girl who works for an accountant will really appreciate this type of copier. Special tax forms printed on one side only on translucent paper are available from most printers. The forms are then filled out in the usual manner by the accountant. These forms are available in three styles:

1. Folded style. This is a large single sheet with printing on one side only. It is then duplicated on a similar large sheet and folded to standard form size.

2. Individual sheet style. Each of the sheets is duplicated separately and then stapled together in proper order. This style can be obtained in pads of identical pages or pads of collated sets.

3. "Flats." These are two strips of translucent paper. Half pages of the official form are printed on each strip. Copy paper that has been sensitized on both sides is used with the strips so that the completed copies are identical to the official forms. Once the flats have been filled in, you place the sensitized copy paper between the strips and place in the duplicator.

Microfilming saves time and space Do you have to go to remote corners of your building in search of records? Are files overcrowded and confused? Perhaps a microfilm machine would simplify your filing tasks and get rid of those cluttered file cabinets.

Microfilming is not difficult, and the equipment is quite compact.

First you have a camera which puts the material on film. One hundred feet of film can copy up to 2500 letters. The material is inserted into the machine, automatically photographed, and returned to you. Only a few seconds are needed for each item.

Of course you will also need a viewer so that you can look up information on the film. This may be combined with a copier so that once you locate the material you want, a picture can be taken and developed for office use.

Microfilming equipment is made by a number of companies.

Automatic typewriters can cut your typing time If there is an automatic typewriter in your office, you may be able to save time on your routine correspondence. These machines can type up to 100 words per minute or 500 error-free letters per day.

With some machines, standard paragraphs that can be used in typical letters are first written and then coded on perforated tape. Each paragraph is numbered. You have a set of corresponding numbers on the control box for the typewriter. Simply push the buttons for the paragraphs you desire and the machine takes over from there. Even if letters must be individually addressed, you still save time with the automatic typewriter since it types the body of the letter much faster than you could by hand. Just type the address and select the buttons for the paragraphs you want. If you have more than one machine available you can go back and forth between them and turn out the work in even less time.

Broken typewriters waste time How much of your employer's work was held up the last time your typewriter broke down? Perhaps if you had been more careful in handling your machine the breakdown wouldn't have occurred. Typewriter manufacturers have these five tips for secretaries:

1. Don't erase over the keys. The eraser dust falls into the machine and causes the keys to stick. Eventually they are thrown out of alignment and have to be reset. This job can hold up work in your office for one or two weeks.
2. When you don't plan on using your typewriter for an hour or more, put the cover on it. Above all be sure your machine is covered before you leave the office at night. Dirt, dust and other foreign matter have a habit of mixing with the oil in your machine to form deposits that finally cause sticking and jamming.
3. Clean your typewriter regularly. Instructions are usually included with each machine. If yours have become lost, drop a line to the manufacturer stating the model you use. Most instructions carry the

phrase "Oil Lightly" and there is a diagram showing the parts to be lubricated. Be very careful that you don't use too much oil and damage the machine. Follow instructions exactly; don't improvise.
4. Develop an even rhythm in your typing so you avoid clashing keys. This causes chipping, which means keys will probably have to be replaced long before their time.
5. Make sure your typewriter is securely placed on your desk. It should never be placed on a drop-leaf or pull-out shelf where it can slide or be jarred from its position.

6

Math Shortcuts

AS A SECRETARY YOU ARE EXPECTED TO HAVE SOME knowledge of basic mathematics. At one time or another you will have to solve problems involving addition or subtraction, or even percentages and proportions. Performed in the usual manner, these jobs can be time consuming. Here are a number of tips to help you speed them up.

Adding with the same number repeated several times in a column When working with payroll accounts, statistics, or averages, you often find the same number appearing several times in the hundreds or thousands column. Use simple multiplication to increase your speed when solving such problems. For instance, if the number 9 appears three times, you need not say, "9, 18, 27," when adding. You know from your multiplication tables that $3 \times 9 = 27$, and you can simply add 27 into the column.

Example: Suppose you are asked to find out how many of a particular item one of your salesmen sold during the last seven weeks. You keep a weekly record of what each salesman sells. Take the appropriate figures from this record, and set your problem up like this:

Items sold during 1st wk:	841
2nd wk:	826
3rd wk:	862
4th wk:	924
5th wk:	965
6th wk:	910
7th wk:	832
Total:	6,160

54 • *Math Shortcuts*

By naming the successive sums to yourself, you found that the total of the column on the right was 20. You carried the 2 to the column in the middle, and added that column. The total of the middle column is 26.

Again you carry the 2, but you notice that the third column contains four 8's, and three 9's. By making the following mental calculations, you can arrive at the total of the third column:

$$\begin{array}{rr} \text{Carried:} & 2 \\ 4 \times 8 = & 32 \\ 3 \times 9 = & \underline{27} \\ \text{Total:} & 61 \end{array}$$

• **suggestion** When you have a very long column, you may have difficulty making these multiplications and additions in your head. You will often find that by using scratch paper for your figuring, you can work more quickly by this method than you can by the conventional method.

Save time with the accountant's method This method is useful when you have to add long columns of figures that contain many digits. Even if your calculations are interrupted when you are in the middle of them, you won't have to waste time starting over. Also, if you suspect that you made an error in adding a particular column in the problem, the accountant's method makes it easy to check that particular column without reviewing the entire addition.

Example: You are asked to find the total volume of sales for your company for the last year. Having a record of the sales volume for each month, you set the problem up as follows:

	Method 1	Method 2
$ 132,456.94	adding left to right	adding right to left
58,241.32		
91,821.26		
246,892.12		
161,232.16	15	44
892,561.40	54	33
120,642.14	43	28
56,223.12	58	56
12,812.56	56	58
238,478.26	28	43
24,840.23	33	54
53,190.23	44	15
$2,089,391.74	$2,089,391.74	$2,089,391.74

Method 1. To add left to right, total the left hand column first. This sum is 15. The sum of the second column from the left is 54. Place the 54 beneath the 15 so that the first digit in 54 (5) is directly beneath the second digit in 15 (5). The next column totals 43, and the 4 of this sum goes directly beneath the 4 of the previous one. So it continues until all the columns are added. The sum of the staggered figures equals the sum of the original column. Once you have the answer, it is easy to get the commas and the decimal point in the right places.

Method 2. To add from right to left, simply reverse the process explained above. Add the right hand column first, and stagger the successive sum in the opposite direction from that used in *Method 1*. Thus, 3, the second digit in 33 (sum of second column from right), is placed beneath 4, the first digit in 44 (sum of right hand column), and so forth.

The accountant's method should not be used for short columns of figures containing only a few digits each. It only saves time when you have to make a very long computation.

Find answers faster by dividing long columns into short sections Another method of adding a long column is to break it up into short sections. This method is especially useful when there are only a few digits in each number. Each of the sections can be totaled, and these sums can be added together to arrive at the final solution to the problem.

The following example shows how to use this method:

```
641
758
910
462      2,771
───
123
892
693
456      2,164
───
810
523
101      1,434
───      ─────
         6,369
```

First, find the sum of the first four numbers: 2,771. The sum of the second group of four numbers is 2,164. The final group of three numbers totals 1,434. The sum of these sub-totals equals the solution to the problem: 6,369.

Learn to add horizontally and save time You are asked to prepare a weekly payroll for a group of salesmen. The payroll is given to you by the day for each salesman. You must find the total week's pay to which each salesman is entitled. You can save a great deal of time by adding the columns horizontally without copying the figures into vertical columns.

Here is the daily payroll:

Salesman	Mon.	Tues.	Wed.	Thurs.	Fri.	Total
Scott, J.	$ 21.10	$ 26.35	$ 18.42	$ 19.90	$20.56	$106.33
Holland, V.	17.26	18.40	23.21	23.60	19.13	101.60
James, F.	27.30	26.20	26.35	25.20	19.46	124.51
Oliver, C.	23.10	18.46	21.45	19.20	20.25	102.46
Taft, M.	22.65	24.30	24.10	23.75	19.16	113.96
	$111.41	$113.71	$113.53	$111.65	$98.56	$548.86

To find J. Scott's salary for the week ($106.33), start with right hand digit of Friday's salary, and add the last digits of each day's salary to it, working from right to left. Thus, you would say mentally:

6, 8, 13.

Put down 3, and carry the 1. Add the second digit from the right for each day in the same manner. Remembering to carry the 1, you would say:

6, 15, 19, 22, 23.

Put down 3, and carry the 2. This process is continued until one horizontal row has been completed. Then the weekly salary for the next salesman is figured.

Method of checking The accuracy of your horizontal addition is easy to check. To do this, you total the vertical columns (find the total salary for each day of the week for all salesmen), as shown in the example. Then find the sum of these totals (add the total daily salaries horizontally to find the total weekly salary for all salesmen). The sum of the weekly salaries of the salesmen should equal this figure. If it does not, you have made an error and should check your work.

In addition to its usefulness on payroll accounts, horizontal addition is a time saver when you work on statistical tabulations, sales records, annual statements, and many other common business problems. The time spent practicing this technique is well worth while.

Three quick ways to check addition results Here are three ways to verify addition:

Add in reverse order. If you originally added a column of figures by starting at the top and working towards the bottom, you can check your answer by starting at the bottom and working towards the top. This is the easiest as well as the most common method of checking addition.

Use the accountant's method. A sum found by the conventional method can be checked by using the accountant's method. If your original addition was by the accountant's method, the sum can be checked by repeating the problem and setting the totals of the columns down in the opposite way from that which was used originally. Thus, if you solved the problem originally by the accountant's method and added from left to right, you can check your result by adding from right to left. If you originally added from right to left, check by adding from left to right.

Check addition by casting out nines. The method of casting out nines is useful not only for checking the accuracy of addition results, but also for checking subtraction, multiplication, and division problems. To cast the nines out of a number, you must first add the digits in the number together. Then divide this sum by 9, and set down the remainder, which is your check number. To cast the nines out of 7,582, first add the digits:

$$7 + 5 + 8 + 2 = 22$$

Dividing 22 by 9 gives an answer of 2 with a remainder of 4. For the purpose of casting out nines, the 2 can be forgotten (the 2 nines are cast out); the remainder (4) is the check number you must remember.

To check addition problems by casting out nines, cast the nines out of each of the figures in the column originally added. The total of the check numbers obtained in this way, once the nines have been cast out of it, will equal the check number obtained by casting the nines out of the answer to the problem.

Example:

7,852	$7 + 8 + 5 + 2 = 22$	Casting out 9's leaves:	4
6,431	$6 + 4 + 3 + 1 = 14$	Casting out 9's leaves:	5
2,578	$2 + 5 + 7 + 8 = 22$	Casting out 9's leaves:	4
9,105	$9 + 1 + 0 + 5 = 15$	Casting out 9's leaves:	6
			$\overline{19}$
		Casting out 9's from 19 leaves:	1
25,966	$2 + 5 + 9 + 6 + 6 = 28$	Casting out 9's leaves:	1

The check numbers 1 and 1 correspond, and you may assume the problem is correctly solved.

- *warning* This method of checking addition is not entirely accurate. In the above example, some incorrect sums (such as 25,696) would have checked out just as well as the correct sum. While the method of casting out nines indicates that an answer is probably correct, it does not guarantee accuracy.

A quick way to subtract mentally It is easy to subtract in your head such numbers as 10, 100, and 1,000. This fact can often be used to advantage in solving subtraction problems.

Before you can use this short cut, you must know that if two numbers are each increased by the same third number, the difference between the numbers as they were originally given is the same as their difference after they are increased. Thus, if you were asked to subtract 4 from 6, the answer would obviously be 2. If you add 6 and 4, and also add 6 to 6, and then find the difference between these sums, the answer is still 2. [12 − 10 = 2.]

Example 1. You are in charge of buying office equipment for your company. A salesman offers to sell you a machine that costs $2,500. He will allow you $750 for your old machine. You want to know how much cash your company would have to pay for the new machine. To find this figure, subtract $750 from $2,500.

You see that $750 is $250 less than $1,000. If you add $250 both to the list price of the machine ($2,500), and to the allowance for the old machine ($750), the difference between these sums will be the same as the difference between the original figures. Therefore, you increase $750 to $1,000, and increase $2,500 to $2,750 in your head. It is obvious that the difference between the increased figures, and hence the cash cost of the new machine, is $1,750. [$2,750 − $1,000 = $1,750.]

Example 2. If it costs $4.64 to ship a package by one transportation system, and $2.36 to ship a package of the same weight by another system, how much more costly is the first system than the second?

You see at once that if you increase $2.36 by $0.04, the new figure is $2.40. Adding $0.04 to $4.64, you find a sum of $4.68. It is much easier to subtract $2.40 from $4.68 in your head than it is to subtract $2.36 from $4.64, and the answer in both cases is the same. It is $2.28 more costly to use the first system than it is to use the second.

Balance accounts quickly and easily When your employer asks you to balance an outstanding account, you probably first add the debits, then add the credits, and finally subtract the smaller of these sums from the larger. However, there is a faster method to balance an account.

The first step is to examine the debits and the credits and determine which are larger. Then total the larger column. Next, leave a blank space (where you will insert the balance) at the bottom of the smaller column. Draw a line under the blank space, and place the sum of the larger column beneath the line. Now all you have to do is add the smaller column in your head, and when you come to the blank space, fill in the number that makes the difference between this new sum and the one you have already written beneath the line.

Example:

Debits		Credits
$ 1,956.18		$ 134.46
3,452.75		258.19
289.34		764.83
5,726.31		2,375.74
$11,424.58	Balance	??.??
		$11,424.58

It is very easy to tell by inspection that the debits are larger than the credits. Just one glance at the thousands in each group of figures shows that there are many more thousands on the debit side than there are on the credit side. Therefore, you add the debits and find they total $11,424.58.

Leaving a blank space (filled in with question marks in the example) at the bottom of the credit column, you draw a line, and place the total debits beneath that line. Now add the credits in your head. The first order (i.e., the extreme right hand column) in the credit column totals 22. Now say to yourself: 22 and 6 are 28.

Therefore, the first order of the balance is 6. Carry 2 to the second order and add again. With the carried 2, the second order totals 22. Say to yourself: 22 and 3 are 25.

The second order of the balance is 3, and you carry 2 to the third order. The third order (dollars) adds up to 23. You say to yourself: 23 and 1 are 24.

The third order of the balance is 1, and 2 is carried to the fourth order.

By continuing this process, you find the balance of the account is $7,891.36.

To give yourself confidence in this method of balancing an account, you might total the credits and subtract that sum from the sum of the debits on a piece of scrap paper. You will find that your balance is the same as the one found above. [$11,424.58 − $3,533.22 = $7,891.36.]

As with all mathematical short cuts, speed and accuracy in using this method will increase with practice.

Two quick ways of proving subtraction   One way to prove subtraction is by addition. If you add the number which you subtracted to your answer, the result should be the number from which you subtracted. Here's how it works:

$5,609.25
− 4,123.05
$1,486.20

The sum of $4,123.05 and $1,486.20 is $5,609.25. Therefore the subtraction is correct.

The other way to prove subtraction is by casting out nines. The system of casting out nines is similar to that used to prove addition problems. (See page 57.) However, instead of adding the check number for each figure in the problem, you subtract the check number of the smaller figure from that of the larger figure. The result should be the same as the check number of the answer.

Here's how it works:

$92,642.63   9 + 2 + 6 + 4 + 2 + 6 + 3 = 32   Casting out 9's leaves: 5
− 84,523.10   8 + 4 + 5 + 2 + 3 + 1 + 0 = 23   Casting out 9's leaves: 5
$ 8,119.53   8 + 1 + 1 + 9 + 5 + 3 = 27   Casting out 9's leaves: 0

Since 5 subtracted from 5 leaves 0, which is the check number for the answer, it can be assumed that the problem is correctly solved.

In some cases, you will find that the check number you are subtracting is larger than the check number from which it must be subtracted. If this is the case, add 9 to the number that is too small:

8,236   8 + 2 + 3 + 6 = 19   Casting out 9's leaves 1; 1 + 9 is: 10
−5,614   5 + 6 + 1 + 4 = 16   Casting out 9's leaves: 7
2,622   2 + 6 + 2 + 2 = 12   Casting out 9's leaves: 3

Learn to multiply by specific numbers This gives you a wide range of mathematical short cuts. In many cases, this knowledge will enable you to multiply easily and quickly without using pencil and paper.

Following are explanations of fourteen short cut methods that involve multiplying by specific numbers. Don't try to learn them all at once. If you learn and practice one method each day, you will know them all in two weeks. If you try to memorize them all right now, you probably won't remember more than one or two of them two weeks from now.

1. *Multiply by numbers that end in ciphers (0's).* First, count the number of ciphers at the end of the multiplier. For instance, there is one cipher in 10; there are two in 100; there are three in 1,000.

Next, add on this same number of ciphers at the end of the multiplicand. For instance, when you multiply 57 × 10, you change 57 to 570.

When the digit preceding the ciphers in the multiplier is 1, this is a very easy multiplication to perform. All you do is add the appropriate number of ciphers to the multiplicand, because multiplying the result by 1 does not alter it. But the system works when other numbers than 1 precede the ciphers in the multiplier.

Suppose you had rented a duplicating machine at a cost of $0.57

a day. You want to know how much the rental will cost for a 30-day period. You use the method described above to solve the problem:

$$57 \times 30 = 570 \times 3 = 1710.$$

By placing the decimal point in the proper place, you find that the rental cost for 30 days is $17.10.

2. *Multiplying by 5.* There are two simple ways to multiply by 5. They are both based on the fact that 5 is one-half of ten.

The first method is to multiply one-half of the multiplicand by 10. Thus, you multiply $9,476 \times 5$ in the following manner:

$$½ \times 9,476 = 4,738$$
$$4,738 \times 10 = 47,380.$$

The second method is the reverse of the first method. You find one-half of the product of the multiplicand times 10. Thus, to multiply 5,739 by 5, you figure in the following manner:

$$10 \times 5,739 = 57,390$$
$$½ \times 57,390 = 28,695$$

3. *Multiplying by 7½.* In order to multiply by 7½ mentally, you must know that 7½ is three-quarters of 10. Therefore, if you multiply a number by 10, and then subtract one-quarter of the product from the product itself, the answer is the same as 7½ times the original number.

Suppose that your employer had driven his automobile 890 miles on company business. The company will reimburse him at a rate of 7½ cents a mile for the use of his car. He asks you to calculate how much money the company owes him. Here is the way you figure:

$$890 \times 10 = 8900$$
$$¼ \times 8900 = 2225$$
$$8900 - 2225 = 6675$$

By properly placing the decimal point, you discover that the company owes your employer $66.75.

4. *Multiplying by 11.* To multiply any number by 11, first write down the multiplicand. Directly below this, write the product of 10 times the multiplicand. The sum of these two numbers is the solution to the problem.

$$\begin{array}{r} 73 \times 11 = 73 \\ 730 \\ \hline 803 \end{array}$$

If the multiplicand contains two digits whose sum is 9 or less, multiplying by 11 is even easier. In this case, you set down the multiplicand, leaving a space between the two digits. You insert the sum of those digits in the space to obtain the product. For instance, suppose that you bought 35 mechanical pencils at 11 cents each. To find the total cost, set down the 3 and the 5 of the multiplicand like this:

$$3 \quad 5$$

The sum of 3 and 5 is 8. Place 8 between the two digits. By properly placing the decimal point, you find that the pencils cost $3.85. Knowing the trick of multiplying by 11 makes it easy to solve this problem in your head.

When there are three digits in the multiplicand, and the last two digits total 9 or less, you can use a modified form of the method just explained to multiply by 11. In this case, multiply the last two digits by 11 in the manner just described, and add to this result 11 times the hundreds figure.

$$\begin{array}{r} 826 \times 11 = 286 \\ 8,800 \\ \hline 9,086 \end{array}$$

The result was obtained by first multiplying 26 × 11, next multiplying 11 × 800, and finally adding the two products.

5. *Multiplying by 15.* To multiply by 15 in your head, first multiply by 10, and then add one-half of this product to the product itself.

Suppose the salary and commission of one of your salesmen averaged $15 a day. You want to estimate what his income will be for the next year (365 days). You multiply 365 × 15 in the following manner.

$$\begin{array}{r} 365 \times 10 = 3,650 \\ \tfrac{1}{2} \times 3,650 = 1,825 \\ \hline 5,475 \end{array}$$

The salesman's estimated salary and commission for the next year will be $5,475.

6. *Multiplying by 18.* The number 18 is 2 less than 20. To multiply by 18 mentally, you first multiply by 20. Next, you multiply the original multiplicand by 2, and subtract this product from the first one you found. For instance, you multiply 780 × 18 in the following manner:

$$\begin{array}{r} 780 \times 20 = 15,600 \\ 780 \times 2 = 1,560 \\ 15,600 - 1,560 = 14,040 \end{array}$$

This is an example of the breakdown method of multiplication, which is useful in many other cases. For a further discussion of this method, see page 64.

7. *Multiplying by 25.* The number 25 is one-quarter of 100. To

multiply by 25, first multiply by 100, and then find one-quarter of the product. To multiply 342 × 25, you figure:

$$342 \times 100 = 34{,}200$$
$$¼ \times 34{,}200 = 8{,}550$$

8. *Multiplying by 35.* The number 35 is the sum of 25 and 10. To multiply by 35, first multiply by 25, and then multiply the original multipicand by 10, and finally add the products.

Suppose that you were going to buy 35 reams of paper at $4.60 a ream. You find the total cost in the following manner:

$$460 \times 25 = 11500 \text{ [See } Multiplying\ by\ 25\text{]}$$
$$460 \times 10 = \underline{\ \ 4600}$$
$$16100$$

By placing the decimal point in the proper place, you discover that the paper costs $161.

9. *Multiplying by 45.* The number 45 is 5 less than 50. To multiply by 45, you multiply first by 50, and then subtract from that product 5 times the multiplicand. Or, since 5 is one-tenth of 50, you can subtract one-tenth of the first product you found from that product itself. To multiply 320 × 45, you proceed like this:

$$320 \times 50 = 16{,}000 \text{ [See } Multiplying\ by\ 50\text{]}$$
$$320 \times 5 \text{ (or } 1/10 \times 16{,}000) = 1{,}600 \text{ [See } Multiplying\ by\ 5\text{]}$$
$$16{,}000 - 1{,}600 = 14{,}400$$

10. *Multiplying by 50.* Because 50 is one-half of 100, to multiply by 50 you need only multiply by 100 and then take one-half of the product.

Suppose your employer owned 4,739 shares of a certain stock which was worth $50 a share. To find the total value of the stock, figure in the following manner:

$$4{,}739 \times 100 = 473{,}900$$
$$½ \times 473{,}900 = 236{,}950$$

The total value of the stock is $236,950.

11. *Multiplying by 75.* Because 75 is three-quarters of 100, to multiply by 75, you multiply by 100, and then subtract one-quarter of that product from the product itself. To multiply 5,684 × 75:

$$5{,}684 \times 100 = 568{,}400$$
$$¼ \times 568{,}400 = 142{,}100$$
$$568{,}400 - 142{,}100 = 462{,}300$$

12. *Multiplying by numbers close to 100.* If a multiplier is slightly more than 100 (102, 103, etc.) multiply first by 100, and then add to

this product the product of the multiplicand and the amount by which the number exceeds 100. To multiply 642 × 102:

$$642 \times 100 = 64{,}200$$
$$642 \times 2 = \underline{1{,}284}$$
$$65{,}484$$

If a multiplier is slightly less than 100, multiply by 100, and then subtract from this product the product of the multiplicand and the amount by which the number falls short of 100. To multiply 642 × 97:

$$642 \times 100 = 64{,}200$$
$$642 \times 3 = \underline{1{,}926}$$
$$64{,}200 - 1{,}926 = 62{,}274$$

This method can be easily adopted to deal with numbers close to 10, numbers close to 1,000, and so forth. It is obvious that the special cases of 9, 99, 999, etc., and 11, 101, 1,001, etc., are especially easy since 1 times the multiplicand will always equal the multiplicand [See *Multiplying by 11*].

13. *Multiplying by 125.* The number 125 is equal to 1¼ × 100. To multiply by 125, you first multiply by 100, and then add one-quarter of that product to the product itself.

Suppose that you purchased 125 boxes of pencils at $4.64 a box. You can find the total cost this way:

$$464 \times 100 = 46400$$
$$\tfrac{1}{4} \times 46400 = \underline{11600}$$
$$58000$$

By placing the decimal point in the proper place, you discover that the total cost is $580.

14. *Multiplying by 180.* The number 180 is 20 less than 200. The number 20 is one-tenth of 200. To multiply by 180, first multiply by 200; then subtract one-tenth of the product from the product itself. To multiply 72 × 180:

$$72 \times 200 = 14{,}400$$
$$1/10 \times 14{,}400 = 1{,}440$$
$$14{,}400 - 1{,}440 = 12{,}960$$

Using the breakdown method of multiplication The breakdown method of multiplication is the foundation for unlimited short cuts in many mathematical problems. The idea behind this method is to break down the multiplier into a group of numbers which are easy multipliers.

Specific examples of the breakdown method may be found on page

62, *Multiplying by 18,* and page 63, *Multiplying by 35, Multiplying by 45,* and *Multiplying by numbers close to 100.*

The key question to ask yourself is "Can I break down the multiplier into a group of numbers that are easier to work with than it is?"

By combining the breakdown method with the tricks of multiplying by specific numbers, many difficult problems become simple problems. Following are two examples that will help you to understand this method.

Example 1. Suppose you were to multiply 564 × 39. The multiplier (39) is equal to 40 less 1. The numbers 40 and 1 are easy multipliers. To solve the problem, first multiply by 40:

$$564 \times 40 = 22{,}560$$

Then subtract 1 times the multiplicand from the product:

$$22{,}560 - 564 = 21{,}996$$

Example 2. Take the multiplier 76. This number equals the sum of 75 and 1. You know the trick of multiplying by 75 (see page 63.) To multiply 564 × 76:

$$\begin{array}{r} 564 \times 75 = 42{,}300 \\ 564 \times 1 = 564 \\ \hline 42{,}864 \end{array}$$

Make multiplication easier with the double and half method The double and half method is based on the principle that if the multiplicand and multiplier in a problem are multiplied and divided, respectively, by the same number, the final product remains the same. Thus if you want to multiply 6 × 2, you can divide 6 by 2, and multiply 2 × 2, and the product of the two answers will be the same as the product of the original problem. The reverse of the procedure also works.

$$6 \times 2 = 12$$

or

$$3 \times 4 = 12 \text{ [Half of 6 times twice 2]}$$

or

$$12 \times 1 = 12 \text{ [Twice 6 times half of 2]}$$

This method of multiplication is especially helpful when a problem involves mixed numbers.

Example 1. Suppose that you had purchased 72 pencils at 2½ cents each. To find the cost you must multiply 72 × 2½:

$$36 \times 5 = 180 \text{ [Half of 72 times twice 2½]}$$

The cost of the pencils is $1.80.

Example 2. The same principle can be applied to solve problems involving other fractions such as ⅓ or ¼. To multiply 217⅓ by 24:

$$652 \times 8 = 5{,}216 \; [(3 \times 217⅓ \times (24 \div 3)]$$

Save time by setting up your own table of multiples Whenever you must do several problems involving large numbers in which the same multiplicand is repeated several times, it is useful to set up a table of multiples.

The first ten in a table of multiples is the multiplicand itself, which is equal to 1 times the multiplicand. To find the second item, which will be 2 times the multiplicand, you add the multiplicand to the first item. The third item, or 3 times the multiplicand, is found by adding the multiplicand to the second item. You construct the table in this manner for the multiples of 1 through 9 times the multiplicand. To verify the table, add the multiplicand to the final item, and if the answer is 10 times the multiplicand, the table is correct.

Example: Suppose your company has one item that sells for $344.76. You know how many of these items were sold each month for the last twelve months. You want to find out the cash volume of sales of this item for each month. You will have to use $344.76 as a multiplicand twelve times. This is how the table of multiples is set up:

Table of Multiples

multiplier		product
1	....	34476
2	(34476 + 34476)	68952
3	(68952 + 34476)	103428
4	(103428 + 34476)	137904
5	(137904 + 34476)	172380
6	(172380 + 34476)	206856
7	(206856 + 34476)	241332
8	(241332 + 34476)	275808
9	(275808 + 34476)	310284
	Verification	
10	(310284 + 34476)	344760

Here's how it works. Suppose the first month, your company sold 4,682 of the items in question. To find the cash volume of sales, you must multiply $344.76 × 4,682. Using the table of multiples, set the problem up in the following manner:

```
           689 52       [2 × 34476]
         27 580 8       [8 × 34476]
           206 856      [6 × 34476]
         1 379 04       [4 × 34476]
         ───────────
        $1,614,166.32
```

The process is repeated to find the solutions for each of the other eleven months.

Use factors to simplify multiplication Factors are those numbers whose product equals a given number. For example, 8 and 3 are factors of 24. Another set of factors of 24 is 6 and 4. Factors of 18 are either 6 and 3, or 9 and 2.

It is often easier to multiply by the successive factors of a multiplier than it is to use the multiplier itself.

Example 1.

$8,642 \times 72$
The factors of 72 are 9 and 8.
$8,642 \times 9 = 77,778$
$77,778 \times 8 = 622,224.$

Example 2.

$9,214 \times 128$
The factors of 128 are 8, 8, and 2.
$9,214 \times 8 = 73,712$
$73,712 \times 8 = 589,696$
$589,696 \times 2 = 1,179,392.$

Using multiplication in the extensions on invoices Making an extension on an invoice is a very practical use of multiplication and a use in which many of the short cuts you have learned will come in handy. When you make an invoice, you are given the quantity of goods purchased and the price per unit. You must find the total cost by multiplication and extend this total cost to the last column on the invoice.

Following is a sample invoice. As a test of your ability to multiply in your head, cover the right hand column of the invoice with a sheet of blank paper, and write down your own answers on that paper. Then move the paper to one side and check with the correct answers.

PETERSON OFFICE SUPPLIES, INC.
1110 Grand Street, Columbus, Ohio 43200

Sold to:
Smith & Brown Co.
47 Bowles Avenue
Columbus, Ohio 43200

Aug.	5	2	Baskets-Wastepaper	@	$1.24	2	48
	8	6	Blotter Pads	@	.79	4	74
	8	8	Pencils-Assorted Color Set	@	1.08½	8	68
	12	15 yds.	Rubber matting	@	2.31	34	65
	12	7	Scissors	@	2.09	14	63
						65	18

Checking multiplication results As with addition and subtraction, the results of multiplication problems should always be double-checked. Here are two alternative methods of checking.

Verify results by division. If you divide the product by the multiplier, the result should be the multiplicand. For instance, to check the problem 73 × 9 = 657, divide 657 by 9. The result is 73, and the problem is proved.

Multiplication results can also be checked by reversing the process described above and dividing the product by the multiplicand. In this case, the result should be the multiplier. To prove the example cited above, divide 657 by 73. The answer is 9, and the original problem is proved to be correctly solved.

Verify results by casting out nines. Check page 57 if you have forgotten the casting out nines method. To verify multiplication results by casting out nines, first cast the nines out of the multiplicand. Next, cast the nines out of the multiplier. The product of the check numbers obtained in this manner, once the nines are cast out of it, should correspond to the check number of the product. Here's how it works:

```
     482         4 + 8 + 2 = 14         Casting out 9's leaves:   5
   × 376         3 + 7 + 6 = 16         Casting out 9's leaves:   7
   2 892
   33 74        [5 × 7 = 35; 3 + 5 = 8]  Casting out 9's leaves:   8
  144 6
  181,232    1 + 8 + 1 + 2 + 3 + 2 = 17  Casting out 9's leaves:   8
```

Using factors in division You have learned how to use factors as a short cut when multiplying (page 67). Because division is simply a reversal of multiplication, factors can also be used as a division short cut. Using successive factors of a number as divisors results in the same quotient as does division by the number itself.

Example 1. A dealer offers to sell you 24 typewriters for $1,349.04 You want to know how much each typewriter costs. Dividing by the conventional method, you set the problem up as follows:

```
          $   56.21
       24 )$1,349.04
              1 20
              ‾‾‾‾
                149
                144
                ‾‾‾
                  5 0
                  4 8
                  ‾‾‾
                    24
                    24
```

If you remember that the factors of 24 are 8 and 3, you can solve the problem more easily as follows:

```
8 )$1,349.04
  3 )$168.63
       56.21
```

Example 2. Your company's delivery truck has been driven 194,256 miles during the last six years. You want to know the average number of miles the truck was driven each month during that period. You know there are 12 months in a year, and hence there are 72 months in 6 years. To determine how many miles the truck was driven each month, you must divide 192,256 by 72. Using the conventional method, you would set the problem up as follows:

```
          2,698
    72 )194,256
       144
        50 2
        43 2
         7 05
         6 48
           576
           576
```

A simpler method of solving the problem is to use the factors of 72, 8 and 9:

```
8 )194,256
  9 )24,282
       2,698
```

Determining the factors of numbers Sometimes it is difficult to determine the factors of a large number by inspection. Knowing the factors, however, can be a great help if you must divide that number into another larger number. Here are some rules that will help you to determine the factors of large numbers:

1. *The number 2 is a factor of all even numbers.* Any number whose last digit is 2, 4, 6, 8 or 0 has 2 as one of its factors.

2. *If 3 is a factor of the sum of the digits of a number, then 3 is also a factor of the number itself.* For instance, the sum of the digits of 8,043 is 15. The number 3 is a factor of 15, and therefore it is also a factor of 8,043.

3. *The number 4 is a factor of any number whose two right hand digits have 4 as a factor, or whose two right hand digits are 0's.* The

number 8,648 has 4 as a factor because the two right hand digits (48) have 4 as a factor.

4. *The number 5 is a factor of any number which ends in either 0 or 5.*

5. *The number 6 is a factor of any even number the sum of whose digits has 3 as a factor.* For instance, 17,892 is an even number. The sum of its digits is 27. The number 3 is a factor of 27. Therefore, 6 is a factor of 17,892.

6. *If 8 is a factor of the three right hand digits of a number, or if the three right hand digits are 0's, 8 is a factor of the number itself.* For instance, 8 is a factor of the three right hand digits (360) of 215,360. Therefore, 8 is a factor of 215,360.

7. *Nine is a factor of any number the sum of whose digits has 9 as a factor.* The sum of the digits of 422,064 is 18. The number 9 is a factor of 18. Therefore, 9 is a factor of 422,064.

8. *The number 10 is a factor of any number which ends in 0.*

Using the rules listed above for determining factors   The use of these rules is best illustrated by example.

Suppose a salesman sold an item for $4.32. At the end of the day he turns in receipts totalling $51.84. You want to know how many of the items he sold during the day. To determine this, you must divide $51.84 by $4.32.

You see at once the sum of the digits is 9. Because 9 is a factor of 9 [$9 \times 1 = 9$], you know that 9 is a factor of 432. (Rule 7) To find the other factors, divide 432 by 9, which gives you a quotient of 48. The factors of 48 are 8 and 6, and therefore the factors of 432 are 9, 8, and 6. The problem is solved in the following manner:

$$\begin{array}{r} 9\overline{)5184} \\ 8\overline{)576} \\ 6\overline{)72} \\ \hline 12 \end{array}$$

In this example you might have determined the factor 6 first rather than the factor 9. Because 432 is an even number the sum of whose digits has 3 as a factor [$4 + 3 + 2 = 9$; $3 \times 3 = 9$], you know that 6 is a factor of 432. (Rule 5) The quotient of 432 divided by 6 is 72. The factors of 72 are 9 and 8. Hence, you arrive at the same factors as you did by the first method.

Solving division problems by the double and double method   The double and double method of solving division problems is similar to the double and half method of solving multiplication problems. (See page 65.)

The system is based on the fact that if both the divisor and the dividend are multiplied by the same number, the quotient remains the same. As with the double and half method of multiplication, the double and double method of division is useful when you deal with mixed numbers. Some examples will explain how the method is used.

Examples: You have spent 28 cents for a certain number of items which cost 3½ cents each. You want to check whether or not the clerk gave you the proper number of items. To do this, divide 28 by 3½. To solve the problem simply in your head, first multiply both the divisor and the dividend by 2, and then solve the problem with these altered numbers:

$$3½ \times 2 = 7$$
$$28 \times 2 = 56$$
$$56 \div 7 = 8$$

Some examples involving other fractions:

$$266 \div 2⅓$$
$$2⅓ \times 3 = 7$$
$$266 \times 3 = 798$$
$$798 \div 7 = 114$$

$$2{,}050 \div 5⅛$$
$$5⅛ \times 8 = 41$$
$$2{,}050 \times 8 = 16{,}400$$
$$16{,}400 \div 41 = 400$$

$$1{,}716 \div 9\tfrac{1}{11}$$
$$9\tfrac{1}{11} \times 11 = 100$$
$$1{,}716 \times 11 = 18{,}876$$
$$18{,}876 \div 100 = 188.76$$

Dividing numbers that end in ciphers The last example above illustrates how to divide by a number that ends in a cipher (18,876 ÷ 100). As when you multiply by numbers which end in ciphers, you first count the number of ciphers. This number tells how many places to the left you must move the decimal point in the dividend. Then divide the altered dividend by the digit (or digits) that precede the ciphers in the divisor.

Example: One of the typists under your supervision typed 740 invoices during the past month (20 working days). You want to know the average number of invoices she typed each day. To find this, divide 740 by 20. Since there is one cipher at the end in 20, move the decimal point one place to the left in 740, changing it to 74.0. Now divide as follows:

Using a table of multiples to divide Suppose you wanted to find the average cash sales of each salesman working for your company for the last year. You know the year's total sales for each salesman. You know that when Sundays, two weeks' vacation, and 10 holidays are subtracted from the number of days in the year, each salesman worked 291 days. Divide the year's total sales for each salesman by 291. The easiest way to do this repeated division by the same divisor is to set up a table of multiples. (See page 66 for instructions on how to set up this table.)

Table of Multiples

multiplier	product
1	291
2	582
3	873
4	1,164
5	1,455
6	1,746
7	2,037
8	2,328
9	2,619

Verification
10 .... (2,619 + 291) 2,910

Suppose the first salesman sold $36,957 worth of merchandise during the year. To find his daily average, divide $36,957 by 291 in the following manner:

```
          $   127
      291 )$36,957
           29 1          [1 × 291.]
           ────
            7 85
            5 82         [2 × 291.]
            ────
            2 037
            2 037        [7 × 291.]
```

Reference to the table of multiples makes it easy to select the proper digits for the quotient, and to accomplish the mechanics of solving the problem.

The process can be repeated for each of the salesmen until the whole problem is solved.

Checking your answers in division One method of checking division is by multiplication. The product of the quotient and the divisor should equal the dividend. To check the problem 35 ÷ 7 = 5, multiply 7 × 5. Because this product is 35, the problem is correctly solved.

A second method of checking is by casting out nines. For an explanation of this method see page 57. To check division results by casting out nines, first cast the nines out of the quotient, next cast them out of the divisor, and then find the product of the check numbers obtained in this manner. When the nines are cast out of this product, it should correspond to the check number of the dividend.

$$\begin{array}{r}525{,}892\\624\ )\overline{328{,}156{,}608}\\312\ 0\\ \hline 16\ 15\\12\ 48\\ \hline 3\ 676\\3\ 120\\ \hline 556\ 6\\499\ 2\\ \hline 57\ 40\\56\ 16\\ \hline 1\ 248\\1\ 248\\ \hline \end{array}$$

Quotient: $5 + 2 + 5 + 8 + 9 + 2 = 31$ Casting out 9's leaves: 4
Divisor: $6 + 2 + 4 = 12$ Casting out 9's leaves: 3
Product of check numbers: $4 \times 3 = 12$ Casting out 9's leaves: 3
Dividend: $3 + 2 + 8 + 1 + 5 + 6 + 6 + 0 + 8 = 39$
                                                       Casting out 9's leaves: 3

7

Where to Find the Answer

AT SOME TIME OR ANOTHER IN YOUR SECRETARIAL career you will be called on for a research job. Many secretaries waste time when they must track down facts, because they don't know where to look for information.

The following list of information sources was compiled to save you time. It is by no means a complete survey but these are sources you will most likely need for business research. Some of these sources should be in your office, ready for frequent use; the others you can probably find at your library.

Atlases
1. *Encyclopaedia Britannica World Atlas.* (C. Donald Hudson, editor) Chicago: Encyclopaedia Britannica, Inc. This atlas contains politicosocial maps, economic, soil and climatic maps, and a gazetteer index.
2. *Hammond's Library World Atlas.* New York: C. S. Hammond & Company, Inc., annually. Here you will find considerable statistical and descriptive data about various regions and countries of the world. There is especially heavy coverage of Canada and Latin America. It also contains United States railway, highway and airline maps as well as full color and black and white maps of the United States and world regions.
3. *Prentice-Hall World Atlas.* (Joseph E. Williams,

editor) Englewood Cliffs, New Jersey: Prentice-Hall, Inc. The final work of preparing this atlas for publication was carried on at the Geographical Institute, Ed. Hoelzel, Vienna, Austria, under the direction of Dr. Hugo Eckelt. It contains 96 pages of colored maps of the countries of the world.
4. *Rand McNally Commercial Atlas and Marketing Guide.* Chicago: Rand McNally & Company, annually. This is a reference compiled with the businessman in mind. It includes highly detailed maps and indexes of the United States and other places; marketing information on state, county and city levels; retail sales maps; and monthly business trend maps and correspondence services.

Business Statistics—Cumulative
1. *Commodity Statistics.* Commodity Research Bureau, Inc. Production, stock, price, and consumption figures are supplied on some 60 commodities. Data includes prices, production, and consumption of these commodities in both the raw and semi-finished state. Figures are carried back for varying periods of years, some as far back as 80 years. This work is helpful for locating trends and markets in previous years.
2. *Commodity Year Book.* New York: Commodity Research Bureau, Inc., annually. *Commodity Year Book* represents an attempt to describe the commodities of commerce. Points covered include statistical tables of price records, production, consumption, and supplies; physical characteristics, methods of production and areas of origin; principal uses; marketing and transportation methods; comparative recent prices; and principal types and grades. It is useful if you need brief information on commodities.
3. *Economic Indicators.* Washington, D. C.: Government Printing Office, monthly. Printed by the Joint Committee on the Economic Report, this publication supplies the reader with a quick look at the current economic situation without his having to look through a large number of specialized publications. The material is presented in chart form and also in tables. Monthly figures are given for the past two years and frequently monthly averages are given back to 1939.
4. *Statistical Abstract of the United States.* U. S. Bureau of Census, Washington, D. C.: Government Printing Office, annually. All the important government statistical agencies are represented, and many of the commonly used private agencies' statistics are included. All sources are given and any changes in method of calculation are indicated at the foot of each table. The "Bibliography of Sources of Statistical Data" is an almost complete list of statistics-collecting agencies.

5. *The Economic Almanac.* New York: National Industrial Conference Board, annually. This brings together a large body of statistics of interest to business and the general public. The "Glossary of Selected Terms" defines in a strictly business sense many of the terms ordinarily found in business reports.
6. *Trade and Securities Statistics.* New York: Standard and Poor's Corporation, annually, with monthly supplements. This service collates a tremendous mass of statistical information. Although the heaviest emphasis is on financial data, there is a large amount of statistical material on general business conditions, cost of living, and prices. The more important Canadian statistics are also included.

Business Statistics—Current
1. *Current Statistics.* New York: Standard and Poor's Corporation, monthly. Indexes of activity in basic industries and production as a whole are furnished each month. Figures on stocks and prices of commodities are also included. This keeps the *Basic Statistics* section of *Trade and Securities Statistics* up to date.
2. *Federal Reserve Bulletin.* Washington, D. C.: U. S. Board of Governors of the Federal Reserve System, monthly. Most of the statistics in this bulletin are financial, but there are also indexes of industrial production, employment, construction, cost of living, and retail sales. The industrial production index is one of the most widely used indexes.
3. *Survey of Current Business.* Washington, D. C.: U. S. Bureau of Foreign and Domestic Commerce, monthly. Indexes of the major fields of business activity are carried on for the current month and the preceding twelve. Each monthly issue analyzes the current business situation and forecasts trends. Usually there are other articles on some new developments affecting business. The biennial supplements consolidate all this information into one volume. A weekly supplement keeps the indexes of production and general business activity up to date.

Dictionaries—Abridged
1. *Funk & Wagnalls' New Desk Standard Dictionary.* New York: Funk & Wagnalls Company.
2. *The American College Dictionary.* New York: Random House, Inc.
3. *Thorndike-Barnhart High School Dictionary.* Chicago: Scott, Foresman & Company.
4. *Webster's New Collegiate Dictionary.* Springfield, Mass.: G. & C. Merriam Co.

Dictionaries—Unabridged
1. *Funk & Wagnalls' New Standard Dictionary of the English Language.* New York: Funk & Wagnalls Company.
2. *Webster's New International Dictionary of the English Language.* 2nd. ed. Springfield, Mass.: G. & C. Merriam Co.
3. *Webster's New International Dictionary of the English Language.* 3rd. ed. Springfield, Mass.: G. & C. Merriam Co. (The Second Edition of Webster's is traditional in its approach; the Third Edition reflects spoken language more.)

Encyclopedias
1. *Encyclopaedia Britannica.* Chicago: Encyclopaedia Britannica, Inc. Articles are, in the main, scholarly, detailed, and well illustrated. They are particularly good for historical and background material, and for general information on the arts, sciences, technology, and political and economic developments of European countries and cities. Yearbooks are published to describe the developments of the year and provide a chronology of important events.
2. *Encyclopedia Americana.* New York: Americana Corporation. The accounts of scientific and technological developments are in general more complete and up to date than those in the other encyclopedias. The descriptions of American cities are particularly good; they give an historical account of their founding, statistics of commerce and manufacturing, and some indication of the cultural and educational advantages available. Each account is followed by a carefully collected bibliography. The yearbooks contain descriptions of important events of the year and keep statistical material current.

Firm Names and Addresses
1. *Kelley's Directory of Merchants, Manufacturers and Shippers.* London: Kelley's Directory, Ltd., annually. Covers in detail manufacturers, wholesale merchants, and shippers of the British Empire. Less detailed coverage on manufacturers of other countries.
2. *Thomas' Register of American Manufacturers.* New York: Thomas Publishing Co., annually. This lists more than 70,000 products, with names of the manufacturers under each product, arranged by state and city. The compilation of trade names and trademarks is excellent for locating the manufacturers of widely advertised products.

Information About Individuals
1. *Who's Who.* New York: The Macmillan Company.   A British publication that gives biographical data on prominent English individuals and some Americans.

2. *Who's Who in America.* Volume 31. Chicago: A. N. Marquis Co.
3. *Who's Who in American Art.* 8th ed. Dorothy B. Gilbert. New York: R. R. Bowker Company.
4. *Who's Who in Art.* London: Art Trade Press, Ltd.   Biographies of leading artists, designers, craftsmen, critics, writers, teachers, collectors, and curators.
5. *Who's Who in Commerce and Industry.* Chicago: A. N. Marquis Co.
6. *Who's Who in Engineering.* 8th ed. New York: Lewis Historical Publishing Co.
7. *Who's Who in Railroading.* New York: Simmons Boardman Publishing Corporation.
8. *World Biography.* New York: Institute for Research in Biography.   This contains short biographies of living world leaders of all callings and countries. The bulk of the material comes from the United States and Europe.
9. *Webster's Biographical Dictionary.* Springfield, Mass.: G. & C. Merriam Co.   This gives biographical material on historical figures.

Quotation Sources
1. *Bartlett's Familiar Quotations.* 13th ed. Boston: Little, Brown & Company.   A collection of passages, verses and proverbs traced to their source in English and modern literature.
2. *Home Book of Quotations.* Stevenson, Burton Egbert, 9th ed. New York: Dodd, Mead & Company.
3. *The Oxford Dictionary of Quotations.* 2nd ed. New York: Oxford University Press.

Reference Books of Facts
1. *Statistical Yearbook; Annuaire Statistique.* Statistical Office of the United Nations. New York: United Nations, annually. This is an annual publication which includes separate tables of all pertinent statistics for all nations of the world.
2. *The Stateman's Year-Book* (S. H. Steinberg, editor). London: Macmillan and Co., Ltd., New York: St. Martin's Press, Inc., annually. The brief tables at the beginning of each volume are useful as a résumé of world production of selected commodities. Each country is briefly described as to type of government, area, population, religion, education, justice, defense, commerce and industry, and finance. The account includes information on weights and measures, coinage, and names the British diplomatic representative within the

country and the country's representative to Great Britain. A brief bibliography for each country is included.
3. *The World Almanac and Book of Facts.* New York: New York World-Telegram, annually. This publication gives tables of statistics on all types of human activity, including manufacturing and production of all types of goods, agriculture, trade, commerce, and banking; résumé of new laws; a chronology of events; lists of United States associations and societies with their addresses and the names of their business managers; government information; postal information; world facts; noted people; memorable dates; astronomical data; sports summaries; and other information.

Regulation of Business
1. *Martindale-Hubbell Law Directory.* Summit, New Jersey: Martindale-Hubbell, Inc., annually. 4 vols. Vols. 1 through 3 contain a list of lawyers and their addresses in the United States and Canada with ratings and other information interpreted by a confidential key. Vol. 4 contains digests of laws of fifty states, Washington, D. C., Puerto Rico, Virgin Islands, and of U. S. copyright, patent and trademark laws.
2. *Prentice-Hall Installment and Conditional Sales.* Englewood Cliffs, New Jersey: Prentice-Hall, Inc., 2 vols., with biweekly supplements. In clear, simple business English, this publication describes the nature of installment sales, the procedure in financing them, the laws and rules that govern them in each of the states of the United States.
3. *Prentice-Hall Labor Relations.* Englewood Cliffs, New Jersey: Prentice-Hall, Inc., 3 vols., with weekly supplements. All Federal and state labor laws are treated fully in this comprehensive loose-leaf service. The full text of each Federal labor law and digests of the state labor laws are provided. The latest decisions, rulings, and opinions by government agencies and officials are reported with editorial explanations and examples. Vol. 1 deals with the Federal Wage and Hour Act and related laws, Vol. 2 covers the National Labor Relations Act and laws related to it, and Vol. 3 covers the state labor laws. Another volume, American Labor Cases, gives the full text of labor court decisions.

Research on Specific Subjects
When you need information on a matter of current interest, your best source will be periodicals—magazines, newspapers, and the like. Fortunately, there are indexes that make it simple to find the article or articles you need. Any large library will have those listed below, and even small libraries will have some of them.

Where to Find the Answer • 81

1. *Applied Science and Technology Index.* New York: H. W. Wilson Company, monthly with quarterly, semiannual and annual cumulations. For the years before 1957 see *Industrial Arts Index*, same publisher.
2. *Business Periodicals Index.* New York: H. W. Wilson Company. Similar to index above, except that it lists articles of a general business nature. Consult the *Industrial Arts Index* for years prior to 1957.
3. *New York Times Index.* New York: New York Times Company, semimonthly with annual cumulations. This is an index of articles in the *New York Times* newspaper.
4. *Public Affairs Information Service Bulletin.* New York: Public Affairs Information Service, weekly, cumulated five times a year and annually.
5. *The Book Review Digest,* published by H. W. Wilson Company, contains a valuation of current literature as reflected in the book reviews included in 80 periodicals of general interest. A descriptive note is given of the book and the names of the magazines in which reviews have appeared, with volume and page number and an indication of the degree of favor or disfavor of the entire review.
6. *The Reader's Guide to Periodical Literature.* New York: H. W. Wilson Company, semimonthly with annual cumulations.

Information on Stocks and Bonds

Three major publishers of securities information, and the most generally useful publications they offer, are given below.
1. Fitch Publishing Co., Inc., 120 Wall Street, New York 5, New York. *Fitch's Monthly Stock Record.* Over 250 pages of statistics on nearly 4,000 common and preferred stocks actively traded on the various exchanges and over the counter.
   Fitch's Bulletin Service. Individual factual analyses of listed and unlisted stocks and bonds, revisions issued four to five times weekly.
2. Moody's Investors Service, 99 Church Street, New York 7, New York. *Moody's Bond Record.* A twice-monthly publication which provides particulars on all types of bond investments.
   Moody's Dividend Record. A semiweekly, cumulative record of dividends and dates of payments and corporate meetings.
   Moody's Manual of Investment, American and Foreign. Annual volumes containing full information about the issuers of the following kinds of securities: Governments and Municipals; Banks, Insurance, Real Estate, Investment Trusts; Industrials; Public Utilities; and Transportation.
3. Standard and Poor's Corporation, 345 Hudson Street, New York 14,

New York. *Standard Corporation Records.* Complete factual information on major American and Canadian corporations and their securities. Six loose-leaf volumes, revised frequently, supply the bulk of the data on balance sheets, earnings, and market prices.
Standard and Poor's Stock Guide. A pocket-size manual devised for quick comparison and selection of investment values in common preferred stocks.
Standard and Poor's Bond Guide. A handbook that presents pertinent comparative financial and statistical information on corporate bonds.

State and Local Government Information
1. *Monthly Checklist of State Publications.* U. S. Library of Congress. Washington, D. C.: Government Printing Office. This lists the more important documents only.
2. *List of Chambers of Commerce of the United States.* New York: Chamber of Commerce of the State of New York, 1951. Lists the names and addresses of each local chamber of commerce in cities of 5,000 and over, arranged by state.
3. *The Book of the States.* The Council of State Governments, biennially. The directory of the states, which is one of a number of sections, gives the names of state officers, the chief justice, officers of the legislature, administrative offices and their incumbents. The names of the administrative offices are especially helpful, for, if the subject under inquiry is known, the titles of the administrative offices practically suggest what office handles the subject. For each state some statistics as to area, population, and other matters are given.
4. *The Municipal Year Book.* Chicago: International City Manager's Association, annually. This is a very comprehensive source of municipal officials to whom you can write.

Trade Associations
1. *Directory of Business Trade and Professional Associations in Canada* Montreal: Canadian Business Magazines. The information contained in this directory is prepared by the Canadian Chamber of Commerce.
2. *Encyclopedia of American Associations—A Guide to the National Organizations of the United States.* Detroit: Gale Research Company. This directory gives a brief description of the organization, the name of its president, date founded, number of members and staff.

Word Books
1. *Dictionary of American Synonyms.* Homer Hogan. New York: Philosophical Library, Inc.

2. *New American Roget's College Thesaurus in Dictionary Form.* New York: Grosset & Dunlap.
3. *Thesaurus of English Words and Phrases.* Rev. from Peter Roget by D. C. Browning. New York: E. P. Dutton and Co., Inc.   With a dictionary you start with a word and find its meaning. With a thesaurus, you start with an idea and find a word to fit it. The basic idea of the thesaurus is its classification of words by ideas—the invention of Peter Mark Roget, more than 100 years ago. A thesaurus gives not only the synonyms of a given word, but *all* related words, phrases, expressions, and opposites in one place, carefully graded according to their fine shades of meaning; and all placed *near* the words expressing the same or similar ideas and concepts.
4. *Webster's Dictionary of Synonyms.* Springfield, Mass.: G. & C. Merriam Company.

Yearbooks and Directories
1. *Ayer's Directory of Newspapers and Periodicals.* Philadelphia: N. W. Ayer & Son, annually. A complete compilation of newspapers published in the United States, Canada and Newfoundland, Bermuda, Cuba, and the West Indies. The arrangement is alphabetical under each state and city. Frequency of publication, special features, circulation, size of page and column width, subscription price, policies and character, and names of editor and publisher are given. It is most useful in the advertising field.
2. *Petroleum Facts and Figures.* American Petroleum Institute, biennially. This publication supplies statistics on petroleum production and the wholesale, retail, and service aspects of the industry.

8

Miscellaneous Time Savers

HERE ARE ELEVEN ASSORTED TIPS YOU CAN USE TO shorten your work day. Don't waste time with antiquated procedures. Get in the habit of using time savers whenever possible.

When you need a substitute What happens when you are sick or on vacation? Can a substitute readily pick up where you left off? If not, she will leave a pile of mistakes that you will have to correct when you return.

The solution is to write out as many of your work routines as you can. Keep this material in a special binder. Try to include samples of completed jobs that can be used as guides. Then if you are sick it will not be difficult for another girl to take over your desk. And when you go on vacation your substitute will find the written samples a welcome supplement to your oral instructions.

Put index labels on your telephone book How much time do you spend flipping through your telephone directory trying to locate names and numbers? Save time by attaching alphabetical tabs at the beginning of each letter. Now you can turn to the letter you want without fumbling or searching.

Speed up your collating Use a rubber finger when collating. This gives you a grip on the paper; avoids slipping, missed pages, and back checking.

A quick way to count cards Often you can avoid the task of counting cards one at a time. Pile up some cards until they measure one inch in height. Now count the number of cards in the pile. If you have 100 cards per inch, then one-half inch would mean 50 cards, one and a half inches would mean 150 cards, and so on.

Correcting wet stencils You don't have to remove a wet stencil from the mimeograph machine and wait for it to dry before making a correction. Simply place a piece of cellophane tape over the error. This will keep the ink from coming through and making an impression on the paper.

Keeping track of your supplies Have you ever been given a last minute job and suddenly found yourself out of supplies? This meant wasted time for you and your executive. Whether you are responsible only for your own desk needs or for keeping the supply cabinet for your department, you need a system for (1) keeping track of supplies on hand, and (2) ordering new supplies. Once you have established your program you can be sure that you will not run out of a vital necessity just when it is needed most. A well-organized program also prevents misplacing supplies, which results in costly re-ordering and delay.

Make a list of all the items you use in your job List each item separately. Be specific; if you simply list *paper,* you will only lose time later when the stationer asks for details. Instead, make entries for *8½ by 11 bond, 8½ by 11 onion skin, 8½ by 11 engraved letterhead,* and so forth. If necessary, include weight or grade, too. Account for every size of paper clip, and for ribbons to fit each make of typewriter in your office.

Double space your list flush with the left hand edge of the paper. Use as many sheets as are needed to complete your supply list. Now rule the paper off so that there are twelve columns (one for each month of the year) following the list of supplies. Then when you are ready to place your order, you can quickly compile a list.

The illustration on page 87 represents a typical page of such a supply list.

Make sure your supply list is up to date Suppose you make your first supply check in January. Consider each supply item individually. Determine how much of each item is on hand. If you do not have a month's supply of an item, note how much must be ordered to bring your stock up to that level. Head the first column following the list of supplies *January,* and enter the quantity you need of each item in that column.

Miscellaneous Time Savers • 87

Item	Jan	Feb	Mar	Apr	May	Jun	Jul	Aug	Sep	Oct	Nov	Dec
Blotters, Desk—Green, 19 x 24												
Blotters, Hand												
Carbon Paper, 6 x 9, Ditto—Master												
Carbon Paper, 6 x 9, Standard wt.												
Carbon Paper, 6 x 9, Light												
Carbon Paper, 8½ x 11, Ditto unit												
Carbon Paper, 8½ x 11, light												
Carbon Paper, 8½ x 11, Standard												
Clips, paper—small—Gem #												
Clips, paper—large—Giant dandy												
Dictaphone belts												
Dictaphone Marking Pad B-68												
Dictaphone Marking Pad B-545												
Dispenser—Scotch tape—Large												

Page of Supplies Inventory File

88 • Miscellaneous Time Savers

You can find supplies faster when everything is in its place Your supply system can only be efficient if your supply cabinet is neatly arranged. You should have a particular space in your cabinet for the storage of each stock item. For instance, you might set aside one or two shelves for the storage of typing paper of various sizes and weights, engraved letterheads, printed forms, and the like. Each item of paper should have its own spot on the shelves.

Type small labels describing each stock item, and attach them to the shelves under the spots where the items are stored. Whenever a new order of an item arrives, place it immediately in its proper place on the shelf.

Save time with printed requisition forms Do you have to write out a requisition each time you need an item from the stock room? Does this involve a description and code number? Why not have a requisition form printed with the most frequently requested items included. Leave a blank space for quantity desired and some space at the bottom for supplies that are only ordered occasionally.

For faster supply delivery—number the desks in your office Are supplies sometimes held up in your office because a new stock clerk doesn't know everyone's name or employees have moved their desks? An easy way to avoid this problem is to give every desk a number. The people may move but the numbers will always be the same.

One person can process all smaller orders when you improve accounting paperwork Do you process many small-quantity orders in an average day? Then it is time you started combining your invoice with the other related shipping documents. Snapout forms are one good method of doing this. If you had snapout forms made up to include a shipping label, packing memo in duplicate, and duplicate invoices, for example, it would simplify typing considerably.

In a typical simplified system, the order clerk receives the duplicate of the shipping memo after the order is sent out. He simply sends out the invoice and files the duplicate by date; the need for a ledger for this information is completely eliminated.

As soon as payment is received, the invoice is taken out of the file and put in the "paid" file. Overdue payments are quickly spotted, since the duplicate is still in the "unpaid" file until payment comes in.

In this system there is no need for the monthly statement, and only on rare occasions are reminders necessary. You save bookkeeping and typing time.

Simplify your reports If you work with reports, consider this fact: a simple report can be read more quickly and understood more easily than a disorganized or untidy one, *and* is quicker and easier to type. Here are some suggestions for simplifying and improving reports you type:
1. Color coding the various sections of a report makes for easier reading (and improves the report's appearance, too).
2. Report headings should resemble newspaper headlines. Make them short and to the point. Readers find what they want faster and preparation of the report is easier when you keep the same headings for each column.
3. Lead-off captions are repetitious and do not help make the report clearer. Try to avoid using them.
4. Use a standard sequence for arranging items on the pages of your report. If you want to make your reports more readable when the number of columns requires an extra wide sheet, place the identifying labels in the middle. Then simply put the figures on the left or right. Since the distance the eye must travel from heading to material is shorter, valuable time is saved.
5. When you want to section off material in a report, use guidelines, gutters (blank spaces between columns), or boxes (a segment of a report enclosed by four heavy lines).
6. Particulars can be easily spotted when you use inverse indentation. This places the important information to the left where it will attract the reader's attention.
7. In order to make the totaling of columns easier in reports containing leadoff captions, use black figures for amounts that add to an item, and red figures for amounts that reduce the item. When adding down, the total of black figures, less those in red, will be the columnar total.
8. Get rid of unnecessary dollars and cents symbols. The people who read accounting reports know what you are talking about.
9. Use tabs and dividers and see that the material is bound in a standard-size cover.

Mail gets out faster when you eliminate envelopes Of course this doesn't apply to normal business letters, but when you are just requesting a brochure or routine information you could use a post card. Some companies now send their monthly statements on post cards. This has proved to be a relatively cheap procedure and a lot less time consuming than the usual procedure of stuffing an endless stream of envelopes.

Specialized services can cut payroll chores A data processing center may be the answer for those payroll preparation headaches. Up till now it was estimated that you needed one person to process a payroll for every 200 employees. Specialists can cut your costs in half.

One company estimates that it saves almost $10,000 a year by using a data processing service. A master card for each employee, containing information on deduction and pay rate items, is prepared and then stored in a processing machine. Timecards and salary authorizations are collected by the service each week. This information is then converted to key punch cards for insertion into the machine. The equipment then produces a check printed with the amount of salary from this background material. Itemized deductions are included on the face of the check.

Each total turned out by the computer is double checked by the service to insure accuracy. Payroll information is recalculated by feeding the punched cards to the computer in a different manner.

Due to constant control and rechecking, this method is considered far more accurate than those involving human calculations. Of course, with the machines the work can be accomplished much faster, too.